I WANT TO BE LIKE YOU, DAD

Breaking Free From Generational Patterns:

Restoring the Heart of the Father

By STAN DEKOVEN, Ph.D.

Stan E. DeKoven, Ph.D.

For information on reordering please contact:

Vision Publishing
1115 D Street
Ramona, CA 92065
www.visionpublishingservices.com
(760) 789-4700

ISBN # 1-931178-39-9

Table of Contents

Forward to the First Edition...5

Forward to the Second Edition 7

Author's Foreword...13

Acknowledgements...15

Introduction..19

Chapter One *The Fragmented Family* 25

Chapter Two *The Story: The Family DeKoven*...................................37

Chapter Three *The Genesis: After Its Kind*..59

Chapter Four *The Biblical Pattern: The Exodus*................................73

Chapter Five *The Demonic Factor* 95

Chapter Six *Recovery: The Way Back* 105

Chapter Seven *Spiritual Warfare*...117

Chapter Eight *Family Forgiveness* 139

Chapter Nine *The Healing*..153

Chapter Ten *Rebuilding Trust*..159

Chapter Eleven *I Want To Be Like You, Dad*....................................165

Chapter Twelve *Secret Places: Hidden Fortresses* 177

Chapter Thirteen *Father God: Rebuilding A Godly Self-Concept*..........191

Appendix 1..211

Appendix 2..222

Non-Christian Spiritual Experience Inventory 238

Addendum..239

Bibliography 243

Additional Information 245

Stan E. DeKoven, Ph.D.

Forward From the
First Edition

How wonderful to see Dr. Stan DeKoven addressing one of the major root problems of warped and wounded people today.

The affirmation, self worth, and blessing that we each receive from our father can literally determine our destiny and success in life.

I have grieved on many occasions to see families derailed through "deadly dads". I remember the car dealer whose whole family joyfully attended our church. Gradually as he prospered, he began flirting with women until he was totally backslidden and engrossed in adultery. When he finally stopped attending church, it wasn't long until his wife and children followed suit. Sadly, the wife became a neurotic alcoholic, and the children ended up on drugs and in jail. That father's pathetic example destroyed his whole family.

God chose Abraham to be our spiritual father in the faith (Galatians 3:29) because he saw that he would make an excellent father, and he would lead his whole family to serve the Lord. (Genesis 18:19)

Many who minister deliverance will tell you one of the predominant roots of demonic problems is rejection, and the source is many times a lack of a father's love. That is why Malachi 4:6 promises God will reconcile fathers to their children to reverse the curses running rampant on earth.

Some statistics indicate that up to 95% of convicted felons hate their fathers and blame them for their warped and wasted lives.

We all desperately need the blessing and affirmation of our fathers. Jesus began His anointed and miraculous ministry only after His

Father said, "This is my beloved Son in whom I am well pleased!" All the patriarchs blessed their children to launch them into their full prosperity and success. Can the blessing be any less important today?

I am overjoyed that Dr. Stan DeKoven has penned a definitive book on how the Lord is breaking this cascading cycle of "fathering failures" by becoming a father to the fatherless and leading the rejected ones out of their chains." (Psalms 68:5-6).

Dr. DeKoven is coming in the "spirit of Elijah" prophesied in Malachi 4:5, and this book is his "thus saith the Lord" to show wounded, hurting, and abused humanity the way back to the tree of life our Lord promised.

Dr. Gary L. Greenwald, Pastor
EAGLE'S NEST MINISTIRES

Foreword From the Second Edition

For years now, the church has been sidetracked with this idea of "Generational Curses." We've watched throngs of Christians swarm to the altars attempting to stop the evil consequences that their forefather's decisions made upon their lives. And... for many years as a pastor, I taught about Generational Curses -- and had seemingly great results. So let's make it clear that we mean no personal disrespect to those sincere people who teach this "ministry." It's just that now... we know a better way (Acts 18:26).

Let's briefly review the teaching of Generational Curses -- it generally goes something like this: "the sins of the fathers pass to the third and fourth generation" (Ex. 34:6-7, Deut. 5:9, Dan. 9:8). This teaching tells how Christians can inherit the attributes or consequences for the sins their predecessors committed generations ago. Sometimes (they say), after the 3rd and 4th generation – the CURSE would be broken... but that part doesn't seem to happen very much anymore.

Anyway, these GENERATIONAL CURSES are said to come from many place, such as follows:

#1 SINS OF ANCESTORS - Supposedly, ancient ancestral CURSES pass down through families. Apparently, Satan has the "legal right" to assault our body or finances because of our forefather's mistakes. They claim these "curses" are why many Christians get sick and die.

#2 WITCHCRAFT/OCCULT CURSES- Sadly, many believe that the words of "witches" have the power to disrupt our lives and affect our surroundings.

#3 CURSES from SPOKEN WORDS- These can be curses spoken by others or by yourself.

#4 CURSES FROM UNGODLY OATHS AND DEDICATIONS/UNGODLY BELIEFS - These "destructive" oaths and dedications could have been made before your birth.

#5 PERSONAL SINS- Your personal perverse sin caused by forefathers same sin.

#6 CURSES PASSED BY IMPROPER TIES (YOKES) - Another BIG teaching concerns "sin in the camp." That's about being YOKED to someone... and inheriting their problems. Somehow you become a "LEGAL target" of all those wretched spirits and "soul ties" that come down their bloodline... to you and your children!!!!!

As far as I can tell, according to this teaching, most Christians are cursed! Apparently, those "legal rights" of the devil cause most of our attacks. And deliverance from these CURSES occurs only when those "legal rights are broken" through effective "prophetic insight," anointed ministry, and prayer. Even though we have not committed any wrong-doing, they say that we can only negate CURSES by public confession and renouncement (speaking utterances) TO THE DEVIL – such as:

"Devil, I cancel all demonic influence that have been passed on to me from my ancestors. ... I renounce all satanic assignments directed toward my family, and me. And I cancel every curse that you or your demon workers have put on me. ... I reject all other possibilities whereby you may claim ownership of me."

Now, these "prayers" to Satan are intended to be said by Christians who already have been "delivered from the power of darkness and translated into the kingdom of God's dear Son." But, that's not all – be very careful – don't get too confident, cuz' another curse may be lurking just around the next corner!

THE REPLY:

Well, some of you already have the answer – before we even get there!! The pagans attempted to pacify capricious "gods" who poured out havoc on humankind for no good reason. For centuries, superstitious people conjured up religious formulas and chanted specific incantations believing that their "magical" words or a particular sacrifice would appease the "unpredictable gods" and forestall misfortune.

THE TRUTH -- WE ARE BLESSED, NOT CURSED:

In the midst of this superstition, the Lord said to Abraham: "And I will make you a great nation, and I will BLESS you... And in you ALL THE FAMILIES of the earth shall be BLESSED" (Genesis 12:2,3). Here we see BLESSING as God's sovereign choice toward ALL believers that desired relationship.

Scriptures say that those who put their hope and trust in God are BLESSED (Jeremiah 17:5). Conversely, those who put their trust in man are CURSED (Jeremiah 17:7). IF we believe, then we are blessed. Do you see? Our battle isn't with the devil... our command is to love God and follow God with all our heart, soul, and might... we are ALREADY BLESSED; regardless of our circumstances. God's not partial. He BLESSES those who believe upon Jesus – (the One who became a CURSE for us) – and we become the beneficiary (heir) of Abraham's blessings (Galatians 3:13,14).

"...Come, you who are BLESSED ... inherit the kingdom prepared for you from the foundation of the world'..." (Matthew 25:34,41). That's our charge... to obtain our blessed inheritance.

NEW COVENANT:

Jeremiah foretold our day (31:28-32) "... People will no longer say, `The fathers have eaten sour grapes, and the children's teeth are set on edge.' Instead, everyone will die for HIS OWN sin... The time is coming, when I will make a NEW COVENANT ,,, it will NOT BE LIKE the covenant I made with their forefathers..." NIV.

Ezekiel knew of the new covenant concerning individual accountability, (read Ez.18:1-4,19, 20), "Yet you ask, `Why does the son NOT share the guilt of his father? Since the son has done what is just and right and has been careful to keep all my decrees, THE SON WILL NOT SHARE THE GUILT OF THE FATHER, NOR WILL THE FATHER SHARE THE GUILT OF THE SON. THE RIGHTEOUSNESS OF THE RIGHTEOUS MAN WILL BE CREDITED TO HIM, AND THE WICKEDNESS OF THE WICKED WILL BE CHARGED AGAINST HIM..." NIV.

JESUS DID IT!

The transition happened at Jesus' death which liberated us from the curse of death... Jesus finished His work. The Scripture is unmistakable on this topic. ... Christ's work was/is sufficient. There's nothing left for Him to do. His salvation is complete. We have His LIFE and we are totally severed from TIES with the devil. We're redeemed from the curse of the law (Gal. 3:13, 4:5) and the influence of sin (Rom. 6:18-23). The curtain of our personal tabernacle was rent.

Yet others teach we're under a CURSE for which we are not personally responsible – because of someone else. And that, my friend, isn't "GOOD NEWS!" This limits the very work that Jesus came to earth to accomplish. To assume that some BELIEVERS who happen to be sick or hungry are under a CURSE – while healthy believers aren't CURSED – is wrong. Not only is this unkind and judgmental -- it's a misuse of scripture.

The fact is, most of us learned inappropriate responses from our environment and family members. For example, my dad was an alcoholic; therefore when growing up, I learned some really bad problem solving techniques. Learned response patterns/habits must be relearned. And, I "renew the spirit of my mind" repeatedly, injecting TRUTH about who God is and who He says I am.

Jesus guarantees our inheritance NOW (Rom. 11:26, 27, Eph. 1:12-14). We're MADE ALIVE in Him (1 Cor. 15:22). Iniquities of previous generations have no LEGAL jurisdiction in the NEW CREATION. Neither do we partake of the sins of our past -- nor the sins of others.

THE DEVIL CAN'T DO IT:

James 4:7 says "Submit therefore to God. Resist the devil and he will flee from you. DRAW NEAR TO GOD..." James didn't say to repeat specific expressions or formulas to the devil about our rights! He can't affect us anymore (see Gal. 3:23-28).

What can separate us from the love of Christ? Not trouble or hardship, persecution, famine, nakedness, or danger. NOTHING. Not past mistakes, words. or curses (Rom. 8:38). "...If God is for us, who can be against us?" (Rom. 8:31). The answer is NO ONE -- NOTHING!) We're delivered from the power of darkness (Col. 1:12-14). Christ FINISHED the work and we sit in heavenly places (Eph. 2:5-6).

Stan E. DeKoven, Ph.D.

CONCLUSION:

For those who live In Christ Jesus, **THERE ARE NO GENERATIONAL CURSES** (see 2 Cor. 5:18-21, Gal. 4:8-10, Tit. 2:13-15). If we believe past failures of our ancestors cursed us, we forfeit the need for personal accountability. We're certainly not "CURSED," but we do need to become accountable. We have "environmental tendencies" -- including inclinations, predispositions, propensities toward wrong behavior, wrong habits, carnality, and negative CHARACTER issues that need to be addressed.

We need to baptize ourselves with the REDEMPTIVE TRUTH that CHRIST lives IN US and we live IN HIM. If we continue to behave badly, then we don't understand the reality our salvation. Being "saved" means to be delivered from the bondage of sin, to be whole, rescued, salvaged, and be in health. Our past repented sins are non-existent. We live by faith in Christ (Gal. 2:10-21, Rom. 5:1-5, Rom. 8:1-8). Ironically, Paul CURSED those who presented a false gospel (Gal.1:9, 4:21).

Out of our own ashes, we emerge as the mature Company -- incorporating the truth that Christ has redeemed us from every curse. Now, with undeserved vindication, we glimpse the nowness of resurrection life and manifest the Image of the overcoming Son.

Kluane Spake
Mind Spring Ministries

Author's Foreword

"He will turn the hearts of the fathers to their children and the hearts of the children to their fathers or else I will come and strike the land with a curse," (Malachi 4:6).

Over the past few years there has been a renewed interest in the person, function and role of the father. It has become readily apparent that there is a distinct necessity to restore the masculine image.

This book examines how the father image has been destroyed in individual lives, and describes how to rebuild a proper father image. You will also come to truly understand God the Father in a deeper perspective, and develop a more intimate relationship with Him.

In preparing to write this book, I thought the most judicious way to discuss generational patterns was to examine the model of my own family life and be willing to uncover some of the skeletons in my own family closet. My personal family history mirrors the world's system, illustrating poor patterns of development and satanic strongholds which can enter into a family's tree and create debilitating problems and dysfunctional life patterns.

Using this approach, I believe you will come to understand the theological and psychological patterns for reconciliation - in the relationship with ourselves and God, and with one another.

There is hope for the family in that I have found that the restoration and rebuilding of the father image is possible; if we are willing to walk the difficult route of being vulnerable. That is; being willing to face ourselves as we really are, and allow the Lord by His Word to transform us according to His pattern.

This book will trace the ways we develop destructive patterns within our family life, and then clearly present the dynamic process of developing new patterns which will lead to liberty and victory in Christ!

Acknowledgements

It is so difficult to acknowledge all the people who have contributed to the development of a concept which has been received by experience and through revelation from the Lord. But I do wish to acknowledge certain special people.

First of all, I need to acknowledge my family whose permission I obtained to discuss the issues and problems that are a part of our family history. They include my mother and father, Ron and Louise DeKoven, my brother, Dave DeKoven, and my sister, Rhonna Porch. Further, appreciation is due to my lovely wife Karen and my two daughters, Rebecca and Rachel, their cousin Alta, and other cousins, Paul and Seth. It is my hope that as you read this book, you will see some of the difficulties of our family tree, perhaps from a positive light, which might bring illumination and healing to your own.

Further, appreciation is due to my lovely, first wife Karen[1], and my two daughters, Rebecca and Rachel, their cousin, Alta, and other cousins, Paul and Seth. It is my hope that as you read this book, you will see some of the difficulties of our family tree, perhaps from a positive light, which might bring illumination and healing to your own.

I would also like to acknowledge the faculty and staff of Vision Christian College and the people of our local fellowship that have endured with me as I have suffered through the development of this manuscript.

I would also like to thank Mr. Michael Wourms whose professional

---

[1] Karen went home to be with the Lord January 24, 2000.

editing of this work has made it significantly more readable. He is a man of immeasurable talent and gifting in the body of Christ.

I want to acknowledge all of the many hurting individuals and families that I have had the privilege of ministering to, and who have started on their road to recovery. I am grateful to have had a part in their healing and restoration. For those to whom I have not been able to properly minister to or help because of my inadequacy, my humblest apologies.

Finally, and most importantly, this work is dedicated to the bridegroom, our Lord and Savior Jesus Christ. May this work be utilized to bring about in some small measure the restoration of His Kingdom.

- "The cat's in the cradle and the silver spoon.

- little boy blue, the man in the moon...

- I wanna be like you dad,

- you know I'm gonna be like you."

- Harry Chapin -

Are we destined to repeat the patterns of our family? Must we walk in the shadow of generations' past?

Stan E. DeKoven, Ph.D.

Introduction

Along with many other leaders who are brighter and more clever than I, It is my belief that we are rapidly moving toward the development of a Church that really will be without spot or wrinkle, a church brought into wholeness in God. Because we are moving closer to the very end of all time, we as the people of God, and more specifically those in leadership, need to be ready to move forward in the power of God, bringing healing and restoration to those who are wounded.

Over the last several years, as I actively ministered to hurting individuals and families within the body of Christ, it has become painfully evident that leaders must experience healing in order to minister healing. It has been well stated (though I cannot remember by whom) that it is not possible to minister effectively above the level of ones own wholeness. Leaders must be willing to experience wholeness, not just to preach or teach about it. Of course, if we are involved in the healing process by reaching out to others, we in turn can be touched by the Lord with His healing power.

The 1980's were characterized as the "me" generation. This was a tumultuous period in which men and women were looking for personal or self satisfaction. This era arrived shortly after one of the most difficult seasons in the history of the United States. Our Western society was characterized by a "free sex, free love, free drugs, no responsibility, do your own thing" philosophy.

In the 90's and now in the 21st Century, the "invoice now due" for that supposedly "free ride" has arrived!

We are now living in the age of the co-dependent, the consummate victim, the dysfunctional, the disrupted and the destroyed. There is a tremendous battle going on within society, and especially the family.

One can readily see how Satan has attempted to destroy the family unit, which is the primary institution of God.

Through the legalistic teaching many Christians have become bound by religious tradition. Other believers, through the extreme behaviors of the past 25 years misrepresented as liberty, have led to severe consequences. We are called to the law of Christ (love?) and not legalism which, when applied to one's life, will create the true freedom to become conformed to the fullness of the image of Christ.

If you have read almost any periodical, secular or Christian, you will find articles on the dysfunctional life. The acronyms: ACA, (Adult Children of Alcoholics); AA, (Alcoholics Anonymous); NA, (Narcotics Anonymous); ACDF, (Adult Children of Dysfunctional Families), etc., within the Church and without have become well known. Researchers claim roughly 90% of the people within the United States suffer from the symptoms of a dysfunctional family, whether they be drug or alcohol related, divorce, separation or abuse.

The truth, as presented so eloquently by Dr. Keith Miller, is that all have sinned, and sin is the greatest addiction that any of us will ever have.

But we have hope... God has provided the answers for us, clearly stated within His Word!

Because of our own individual orientation or lack of knowledge, many have failed to apply His answers universally to bring liberty to the captives. As we read the scriptures, some may see a seeming inconsistency between the concept of salvation as a cure versus salvation as a process.

This is because salvation is an event <u>and</u> a process. It is a process of changing, growing and becoming all that God has intended us to be.

In the 90's and beyond, as we face the onslaught of dysfunctional families, codependents, dependency on alcohol and drugs, etc., there is a greater need for a clear understanding of the plan and power of God. We must search for answers; truths which will lead people to real liberty in Christ! Jesus came to liberate those who were in bondage.

His power is sufficient.

This book is for souls who are seeking a rational and relational healing. It is for those who are hurting and are looking for hope and a release of God's power, thus facilitating the process of restoration. These souls are tired of doing the same old thing, of applying psychological techniques to their spiritual life. They are tired of simply being prayed for and then turning around and walking away from the altar the same as they were when they came.

This book is for those courageous souls who are searching for a tool to break the chains of bondage as they counsel others. It provides the necessary tools and techniques for counseling the wounded, and will become an important resource for strugglers. Hopefully, this book will assist them in grasping the plan, purpose and process God has ordained for their journey to wholeness.

Finally, this book is written to the Church, especially to the leaders in the Body of Christ. In Malachi 4:5, the scripture states that before the restoration of the hearts of the fathers to their children, and the children to their fathers, the spirit of Elijah would be sent by God the Father. This outpouring of the Spirit of Elijah was first seen in the ministry of John the Baptist.

John powerfully and forthrightly confronted the sin of his generation. Every generation must confront --through spiritual warfare -- the spirit of the age, which is characterized by self-centeredness, pride, lack of true compassion, and the pursuit of selfish needs rather than the good of others. The spirit of Elijah is a spirit of confrontation and of presenting the truth of the Gospel without compromise. The spirit of Elijah is coming to the Church and is desperately needed to eradicate the spirit of this age and bring restoration to the precious wounded.

My prayer is that we may we be open and vulnerable, healers of the wounded of our generation – perhaps the last generation before the consummation of all history, beginning with ourselves.

Dr. Stan E. DeKoven

It is a reverent thing to see an ancient castle or building not in decay: or to see a fair timber tree sound and perfect. How much more to behold an ancient and noble family which hath stood against the waves and weathers of time.

- Sir Francis Bacon: Essays -

Stan E. DeKoven, Ph.D.

Chapter One

The Fragmented Family

The dysfunctional family is the disease of today's society. Over the last several years, we have seen the development of numerous kinds of self-help groups designed to bring healing and restoration to those who have been broken through the ills of our society. These societal ills include (but are not limited to) alcohol and drug abuse, a 50% plus divorce rate, domestic violence and those stresses brought about by poverty and racism.

Until recently, the Church has been dormant. Now, they have joined the bandwagon of the self-help movement. Much good has come from this as churches have recognized the responsibility to minister to those who are hurting.

Yet, as is often the case, the Church moves forward with little or no conscious recognition of God's plan, His design, His purpose and His objective. God desires to fill up (bring to fullness) all things in Christ and to develop the Church, the Body of Christ, to become whole and complete in preparation for the coming of the Lord.

God is definitely restoring His church! But, in order to restore the Church, the individual people of the family of God must be restored. Eventually, the nations must be turned, through the Gospel of Jesus Christ, to righteousness and holiness. As many of the prophets of our day have echoed, "it's a time for the healing of the breech," which is spoken of in Isaiah 58:12 (NIV).

> *"Your people will rebuild the ancient ruins and will raise up the age-old foundations; you will be called Repairer of Broken Walls, Restorer of Streets with Dwellings."*

It is now the time to see the brokenness in relationships healed and individuals restored in preparation for God's end-time move!

To bring restoration to broken places, the patterns human beings live by, whether they be functional or fragmented, must be examined and understood. It is essential to observe them from both a Biblical and a psychological/social viewpoint. Beginning with generational patterns, we are going to see how the symptoms of dysfunctional behavior are passed on from generation to generation. We will observe in the spiritual realm how generational curses or patterns of negative, maladaptive thoughts, emotions, beliefs and behavior are transmitted from generation to generation.

Along with reviewing and analyzing these patterns, biblical truths will be brought to light to facilitate the process of healing and restoration provided to individuals and the Body of Christ via the power of God. Using God's Word, prayer and spiritual disciplines, negative patterns, iniquity of the fathers, or "curses" will be broken, new wholesome patterns will be reestablished, leading to more effective and purposeful living. The problems the Church is facing today seem overwhelming. In spite of what is seen, the reality is that all things are in the Father's control.

The Lord can be trusted to afford mankind with the answers vitally needed to provide necessary direction to produce healing and restoration for the wounded in the Body of Christ. To begin our understanding, there are three questions often posed by someone raised in a dysfunctional family:

1. Who am I?

2. What is my purpose?

3. What must I do to be safe?

These questions must be resolved for an individual to be able to fulfill our destiny in God. To each of the questions there are varying sincere responses. They range from the material to the spiritual, from the ridiculous to the sublime. The following represents a review of some of those responses:

Who Am I?

I am what I eat, or my life is my physical existence, and the length of my life and the health of my existence is most important. Thus, I am what I feel, how I look, or how I compare to others in my sphere of influence.

Others, especially men (though this is changing some) will state, "I am what I do." Their work or especially their title determines their relative worth. This distortion of true identity is not just seen in secular circles, but in the image enhancement demonstrated by local pastors who exhibit 9 or more letters after their names (B.A., M.A., Ph.D., etc.). Education is an important ingredient for successful ministry, but it should not be the primary basis of self-esteem.

Related to education as image enhancement is, "I am of worth because of who I know, where I live, how much money I have, etc." All of these identity enhancers, if portrayed as a primary statement of worth, are fleeting at best. Yet, they are quite commonly the "masks" worn by many.

Finally, and this is especially true for men and women raised in dysfunctional homes, "I am" what has been spoken over me from times past. These "prophetic" words make up the "compensations" for the true identity which Christ will form in us and are the focus of this book. Our identity, or our core self-concept is primarily formed by age 8-10 years. If one has been told that they are ugly, stupid, inferior, whether in word or deed (or both), over a period of time, by a significant other (usually a parent and especially a father), that label becomes indelibly etched into consciousness. Essentially these negative prophecies when embraced distort the Godly self-image causing permanent, if not irreparable damage. These images are reinforced through chosen (whether unconsciously or consciously) adult relationships, and patterns (especially co-dependent or dependent) develop.

Any one of the "I am's" covered here will leave a hole in the soul that needs filling with something. The attempt to meet deeply felt and legitimate needs through self-medication, compulsive behavior, or passive avoidance will never work, but may give temporary relief from shame based (I am worthless, I will never make it) identity. The church must be prepared to minister to the core identity of God's people, and bring more than symptomatic relief. The heart cry is for actual restoration of the heart or core of the person.

What is My Purpose?

Productive and purposeful activity is one of the essential elements of a happy and well adjusted life. Somewhat related to one's identity, or an extension of it, is a person's unique purpose. "What is my life all about and what am I here for?" These are not merely adolescent questions, but questions of the aged as well.

Purpose is related to vocation. In secular terms, our vocation is that which will provide for necessary status, esteem, comfort, and security. As such, the greater one's status, education, vocation, the greater their worth in this world. The Church of Jesus Christ has a distinctly different perspective.

Essentially, to the committed Christian, vocation means servant hood to Christ and His Body. A Christian's avocation is that which we do to pay our bills. Within that purpose, the highest calling would therefore be that of five-fold ministry, or to other service (Elder/Deacon) in the local assembly. The church has strayed far from these lofty goals to accommodate the world's perspective of worth.

What Must I Do to be Safe?

Since the vast majority of Western civilization has been raised in dysfunctional families, where boundaries have been severely violated, the desire for safety and security is a real heart cry. This need has been exacerbated since the tragedy of 9/11. The need for a sense of safety is necessary for growth and individuation or actualization. However, the traditional route recommended by most to attain this safety is diametrically opposed to the Word of God.

Conventional wisdom dictates that we must find ways to preserve one's life, protect one's space, conserve one's energy, serve one's own highest good. Whether through self-help groups (much good has come from them), outpatient psychotherapy, or self-help books, the focus has been on teaching a dysfunctional family member to love, nurture, and protect himself or herself, and reestablish boundaries where betrayal has occurred.

No doubt, self-acceptance is necessary, and healing from the wounds received is essential for growth to occur. However, dangerous self-preoccupation has frequently been the result. It is essential to grow beyond the goal of one's primal safety, and to recognize the Biblical mandate for all believers. Christ has called all of us to follow the road that our Messiah walked, which included the sacrifice of His self (death) so that His resurrection life could flow through others.

A closer look at Christ's plan for deliverance and restoration will provide clarity to this discussion.

Christ's Plan

In Isaiah 61 and Luke 4, the plan of God for our liberation from the bondage of sin is described. It is through the Anointed One (Christ) and the abiding anointing (the Holy Spirit) that mankind's healing will come. An examination of the primary truths found in each passage is most appropriate as an explanation of God's restoration and healing power for the body of Christ.

The Prophecy

The Spirit of the Sovereign LORD is on me, because the LORD has anointed me to preach good news to the poor. He has sent me to bind up the broken-hearted, to proclaim freedom for the captives and release from darkness for the prisoners, to proclaim the year of the Lord's favor and the day of vengeance of our God, to comfort all who mourn, and provide for those who grieve in Zion - to bestow on them a crown of beauty instead of ashes, the oil of gladness instead of mourning, and a garment of praise instead of a spirit of despair. They will be called oaks of righteousness, a planting of the LORD for the display of his splendor. They will rebuild the ancient ruins and restore the places long devastated; they will renew the ruined cities that have been devastated for generations. Aliens will shepherd your flocks; foreigners will work your fields and vineyards. And you will be called priests of the LORD, you will be named ministers of our God. You will feed on the wealth of nations, and in their riches you will boast. Instead of their shame my people will receive a double portion, and instead of disgrace they will rejoice in their inheritance; and so they will inherit a double portion in their land, and everlasting joy will be theirs. For I, the LORD, love justice; I hate robbery and iniquity. In my faithfulness I will reward them and make an everlasting covenant with them. Their descendants will be known among the nations and their offspring among the peoples. All who see them will acknowledge that they are a people the LORD has blessed. I delight greatly in the LORD; my soul rejoices in my God. For he has clothed me with garments of salvation and arrayed me in a robe of righteousness, as a bridegroom adorns his head like a priest, and as a bride adorns herself with her jewels. For as the soil makes the sprout come up and a garden causes seeds to grow, so the Sovereign LORD will make righteousness and praise spring up before all nations," (Isaiah 61:1-11).

The Fulfillment

"The Spirit of the Lord is on me, because he has anointed me to preach good news to the poor. He has sent me to proclaim freedom for the prisoners and recovery of sight for the blind, to release the oppressed, to proclaim the year of the Lord's favor," (Luke 4:18-1).

Comments

In the prophetic pronouncement found in Isaiah 61, the prophet foretells of One who will come who has the full measure of the Spirit of the Lord upon him. His primary focus of ministry will include the proclamation of the Good News. The Good News is embodied in an Anointed One (set aside, sanctified, consecrated, also unction or flow of power) who has the power of God to proclaim the Good News. The Good News is that the brokenhearted can have their broken hearts mended, that those imprisoned by sin and the roots of shame, bitterness, rejection, etc., can be liberated and experience freedom. The prophet proclaimed that the year of Jubilee (freedom, rejoicing) is now and will forever be because of this Anointed One!

Further, Isaiah declares that all of mankind's joy would be made full because of the justice of our God, including the punishment of the wicked (unrepentant).

This proclamation is so powerful, so full of excitement and so incredible, it almost seems too good to be true! But, for those who have ears to hear and a heart to receive, it is assuredly Good News.

When Jesus stood in the synagogue at Nazareth, He laid claim to and accepted ownership of the anointing Isaiah had promised. His life echoed the validity of this prophetic word. Jesus further identified His Messiah-ship by proclaiming a message of hope to the poor, and sight to the blind (physically, soulishly and spiritually). His statement concerning the downtrodden reflects Isaiah 61:2c-3 where He promises comfort for those who mourn.

The losses commonly experienced in life, the rejections endured, the betrayals too frequently suffered create a brokenness that remains buried within until release comes. For those who mourn, comfort is and will be provided. But for those who <u>never</u> mourn their losses - personally, in family or corporately (in their Church or nation) - there is no comfort to be received.[2]

The promise to the down trodden, to those suffering from loss, is a garland (a wreath of victory) because of Christ's triumph over death. It is the oil of gladness (the Holy Spirit as Paraclete or comforter), and praise which will sustain a believer as the grief process is experienced. Furthermore, as one progresses through their unique (yet common) hurts and bitter disappointment, a new identity (Godly self-respect, trees of righteousness) and a new root system emerges.

Instead of bitterness, a believer can be rooted and grounded in the love of God through Christ! This is His promise.

What continues in Isaiah 61 are the <u>results</u> of willing submission to God's process of cleansing, deliverance, reconciliation and restoration. What a wonderful promise hinges upon the small word "then."

<u>Then</u> will one see the rebuilding and repairing of the desolation (ruin, waste) brought upon this generation, a result of sin and rebellion.

---

[2] See *Grief Relief* by Dr. Stan DeKoven.

Then will the world see the results of the handiwork of God in the restored's life.

Then the formerly wounded will be called God's priests and ministers, and enjoy His blessings instead of shame.

The restored's joy will be double.

The shame and humiliation will be removed.

Believers who appropriate the promise of God found in this passage of scripture will possess the possession of God and take their place as blood washed saints, wrapped in the robe of His righteousness, and take their rightful place, not a second hand Rose, but as part of the Bride of Christ, without spot or wrinkle. This gives to all hope instead of despair. If it were not for these precious promises of God, fulfilled in the risen Lord, there would be no hope for any of God's creation.

Through Christ, all believers are able to experience, over time, this victory.

First, comes the acceptance of the Good News.

Second, comes the mourning which leads to comfort.

Finally, comes the new identity which leads us to a total participation in life as God intended for us. The working out of this perfect provision of Christ is easier said than done, but for those willing to continue on the journey, Christ's promise will be fulfilled.

The promises of God found in His Word are absolute, powerful and available to all His children. The appropriation of God's promises to the "real world" is a difficult process, but, as will be presented in this book, can be appropriated through a consistent application of His Word over time. An example from a family dear to my heart will begin to illustrate the process.

Civilization varies with the family, and the family with civilization - Its highest and most complete realization is found where enlightened Christianity prevails; where woman is exalted to her true and lofty place as equal with the man; where husband and wife are one in honor, influence, and affection, and where children are a common bond of care and love. - This is the idea of a perfect family.

- William Aikman -

Chapter Two

The Story – The Family DeKoven

I remember making a vow when I was a young man in my early twenties. The vow was to myself and anyone within earshot. I promised, to the best of my ability, that I would never, ever, ever become like my father!

Many have made similar vows - to do whatever we can to avoid the negative patterns we observe in our fathers or mothers, hoping to then change the circumstances and situations of our life.

If the truth be known, most people can recognize the similarities only too well between oneself and the significant members of one's family of origin. In my case, I was the second-born child, the first son in a family with three children. My earliest recollections were of a fairly secure family situation until about age 5 when my parents separated for about 3 months (it seemed like nine!).

After that separation, my family came back together and my early school experiences were within the "normal" ranges of most children living in the inner city. My earliest memories include a deep desire to achieve something of worth in my life.

I was somewhat of a loner, fairly easily hurt, and yet always coming back for more, looking for approval, love, security and significance from my family. I became an over-achiever from the age of 8 both in sports, and in scholastics.

I desperately wanted to please, to find approval from those around me. Of course, I was not always successful in my pursuit.

In our family, education was seen as very important, yet my parents, because of their lack of education, felt they could not be much of a role model for me. My sister, 4 years older than me, was a fairly good student until junior high where she became much more socially oriented (academics became a secondary pursuit). My younger brother, considered the baby of the family, was sickly as a child but became a primary playmate and antagonist for me.

In my family system, trying to be approved and to find a sense of security, was a constant, everyday battle. My growing up was spent outside of the family. I preferred to be with neighbors and friends, playing baseball, seeking to have a deep need met in my life for the love and security I was unable to receive in my family of origin.

I became a Christian at the age of twelve. Shortly thereafter I received a powerful and distinct call of God on my life. After this most profound and life changing event, my journey went in numerous directions. My primarily was focused on surviving the educational system and preparing for a baseball/ministry career. As with most young people, I had a limited concept of my future, or who to achieve my lofty goals. I had little or no guidance in the decisions I made.

By the grace and mercy of God, I was ultimately able to complete my college education and graduate studies, and I developed a modicum of success by the standards of the world and the Church. Still, within my heart, I carried a deep need for connectedness, for belonging, for understanding who I was. Nagging questions remained, the chief of which was, "Why did I do certain things that were directly opposed to what I knew was best for me."

For example, I did not quite understand why certain temptations were virtually overpowering for me. It was more than just hormones that came upon me in the difficult area of sensual desires. This affected my various desires, hopes and dreams, and even the way I responded to stress.

In my psychology studies, I recognized that most of the patterns I had learned came from my family of origin. Yet, some of the patterns seemed to come from somewhere beyond my family life. These issues seemed unexplainable and diabolical, and I had little ability to overcome them. My faith in the Lord and His Word was strong, yet the struggles were so difficult, and so I often failed.

God has created us to be overcomers, yet, most Christians are, as the scriptures teach, broken reeds and burning flax.

But God's overcoming power is available to all!

> *"Going on from that place, he went into their synagogue, and a man with a shriveled hand was there. Looking for a reason to accuse Jesus, they asked him, 'Is it lawful to heal on the Sabbath?' He said to them, 'If any of you has a sheep and it falls into a pit on the Sabbath, will you not take hold of it and lift it out? How much more valuable is a man than a sheep! Therefore it is lawful to do good on the Sabbath.' Then he said to the man, 'Stretch out your hand.' So he stretched it out and it was completely restored, just as sound as the other,"* (Matthew 12:9-21).

> *But the Pharisees went out and plotted how they might kill Jesus. Aware of this, Jesus withdrew from that place. Many followed him, and he healed all their sick, warning them not to tell who he was,"* (Matthew 12:14).

This was to fulfill what the prophet Isaiah spoke:

> *"Here is my servant whom I have chosen, the one I love, in whom I delight; I will put my Spirit on him, and he will proclaim justice to the nations. He will not quarrel or cry out; no one will hear his voice in the streets. A bruised reed he will not break, and a smoldering wick he will not snuff out, till he leads justice to victory. In his name the nations will put their hope,"* (Matthew 12:18-21).

Christ has not discarded His children! In fact, God has embraced His chosen ones bringing them into the fullness of the kingdom of His dear Son, into the kingdom of light and love.

As a young man, I searched in several directions for answers to how the patterns of my life, both good and bad, were developed. This became a search to understand myself so that I could better understand others and their search for wholeness and completeness in God.

I reviewed philosophy.

I explored psychology in depth.

I studied religion, and inquired into church life.

I began to seek the Lord with a diligent heart. My search finally has brought me to the discovery of biblical principles that, when properly applied through knowledge, wisdom and the power of God, will bring release. These principles gave have given me hope for breakthrough and movement toward the position of restoration of relationships in my family and with the Lord.

Up the Family Tree

A fairly well-known psychiatrist, Salvador Minuchin, developed a theory for the development of psychological problems that he calls the multi-generational family transmission system of psychopathology. What a mouthful!

In simplified form, Minuchin observed (and many scientists have confirmed) that the patterns of family life are learned, including communication style, specific problems, belief systems and attitudes toward themselves and others. These patterns are transmitted via the communication process and modeling.

Over generations, symptoms including the pathological or dysfunctional aspects of personality, behavior, thoughts, beliefs and attitudes are also transmitted from generation to generation. Minuchin and others discovered that the family pattern, whether functional or dysfunctional, are observed in a family's tree over 3 to 4 generations.

In Exodus 20, Exodus 34, and many other places throughout the Word of God, it says that the sins (or iniquity, to be defined later) of the father (generations) are transmitted unto the 3rd and 4th generation to those who hate God.

> *"You shall not bow down to them or worship them; for I, the LORD your God, as a jealous God, punishing the children for the sins of the fathers to the third and fourth generation of those who hate me,"* (Exodus 20:5).

In my family, I have observed some interesting patterns of behavior that are clearly outlined in my family tree. In family counseling, therapists frequently utilize a tool called a "genogram" to outline the history of a family.

I have provided a simplified genogram of my family in figure 1. As can be seen from the illustration, my family tree, traced back to the 4th generation, carries a number of interesting beliefs, attitudes and symptoms which have been exhibited in one or both of my siblings as well as myself. This is documented by our family history.

In this chapter, one will observe through the eyes of my family tree; a rose by any other name still has thorns. Perhaps I was raised in such a family for just this very thing. Virtually every symptom one could ever have can be found within my family background. Thus, as is recommended in the Word of God (I Corinthians 15:46) a look at the Family DeKoven, or the natural first, as the type for how the generational pattern develops will be presented.

This will also illustrate how various problems and concerns can be transferred from generation to generation through communication and learning. Finally, a full review of the biblical and spiritual dynamics involved will show just how the generational pattern or the iniquity of the generations can be brought upon families (even upon families that have been born again and spirit filled. The purpose of which is to show who these patterns develop, and to provide a clear prescription for overcoming the difficulties caused by the generational problems.

Like Father, Like Son!

Yasel's Yarn:

First we are going to look at my father's family tree. We begin with my great grandfather Yasel Cohen. Yasel was a Levitical Jew (non practicing), who was a most interesting gentleman. According to my father, he was a very gregarious, happy-go-lucky individual who was barely 5' 2" and weighed over 240 pounds. Yasel was an aggressive man who had a great desire to care for his family. He was initially an immigrant from Poland with a Jewish heritage.

Yasel married a young woman from Norway. They had a son named Stanley Harry Cohen. Shortly after Stanley was born, Yasel and Ms. Undum divorced, and young Stanley was told his father was dead (This leads to an interesting family story discussed later).

Yasel had many difficulties in his life, but he never had difficulty obtaining money. He was very good at it. The way he got money, however, was not always considered in the best interest of those with whom he did business.

Specifically, Yasel had a propensity toward marrying women, especially women with an excess of money and a lack of sense!

Further, Yasel was not beyond extorting money for his own benefit, and may have had some underworld connections. Considered a gentle man, he was nevertheless far removed from any religious connection to Father Abraham.

Figure 1

THE DEKOVEN FAMILY

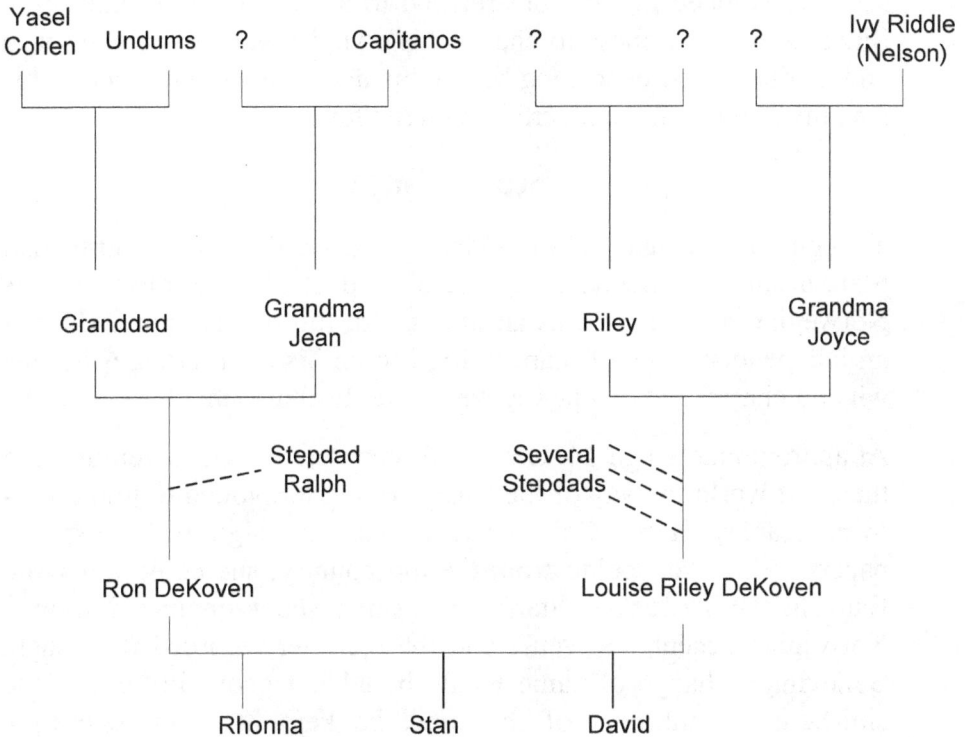

Yasel Cohen	Undums	?	Capitanos	?	?	?	Ivy Riddle (Nelson)

Granddad   Grandma Jean   Riley   Grandma Joyce

Stepdad Ralph   Several Stepdads

Ron DeKoven   Louise Riley DeKoven

Rhonna   Stan   David

My father relates that my granddad Stan, my namesake, had not known his father, Yasel. His Norwegian mother had thrown Yasel out of the house and divorced him (no doubt for dubious behavior on his part), and told granddad often that Yasel was dead. After Stan was grown and married, my father, Ron, was born. Yasel paid an unexpected visit to see his son and grandson. When they saw each other at the front door of the family home, Stan asked who he was. When Yasel responded, "I'm Yasel, your father," Stan fainted and fell to the floor!

It was probably the only time my granddad was "floored" about anything.

Yasel was an adult onset diabetic who died at the age of 74. He had severely stubbed his toe, but refused to allow anyone to help him. Since he was too obese to change his own dressing, gangrene set in and he died. However, long before his death he had imparted to his son, my granddad, Stan, certain patterns for living.

Stan's Saga

Though I never met great grandpa Yasel, I did know my granddad Stan, a colorful character. Being a child of divorce, raised by his Norwegian mother, he was an only child, full of adventure. He was an independent type of man, living life on his own terms, using his wit and charm, and displaying considerable chutzpah.

At approximately age 14, Granddad Stan determined to venture into the adult world by way of the Navy. Being too young to join on his own, Stanley Harry Cohen had his mother sign his enlistment papers. However, being from the old country, she could not write English. When asked Stan's last name, she pronounced it in a Norwegian accent, "Koven", and the recruiter recorded it as such. Believing a change of name would be advantageous in light of the anti-Semitic sentiment of the time, he kept it. Later, due to a fascination with Mexico and Spanish surnames, and at an opportune time (to avoid trouble with the law), put the "De" in front of the Koven.

Therefore when you think of me, remember, my name is fictitious!

While in the Navy, my grandfather learned the skill of diplomacy as a corpsman. He married my grandmother, Demetria (Jean) Capitanos, and they had one son, Ronald Stanley DeKoven.

After leaving the Navy, granddad Stan had a variety of jobs, including car salesman, bartender and seller of beach front property in Arizona! He also "ghosted" as a building contractor, and was a fortune teller for a season.

My grandfather had little patience for children, so his skill as a parent was rather limited.

My father was raised in a home of little genuine love, much abuse and neglect. Granddad Stan divorced Grandma Jean when my dad was about 10 years old. He remarried and divorced again, but never lacked the companionship of people. He died at 67 of heart disease. He was an alcoholic, and a good Lutheran.

My Grandma Jean was no innocent victim of Granddad Stan's propensities. She could "hold her own." Coming from Greek lineage, she was quite passionate, though often manipulative and controlling. All three of the "Wig sisters" (my two aunts and Grandma Jean) had difficulty letting go of their sons and were jealous and competitive to the very end. The results of my father's environment included extreme anger, divorce, infidelity, dishonesty, and other difficulties. Before looking at my father, let's take a peak at my mom's family tree.

Really Riley

Much less is known about my mom's family, especially my mom's father, whom she barely knew. We only know his name is/was - Riley, and he was of Irish extraction.

Consistent male role models were rare in my mom's family.

My grandma Joyce was also an interesting character. My mom's grandmother, Ivy Riddle (Nelson) was married to Thomas Jones. She also had three brothers; Roy, Red, Tony Nelson. Grandma Joyce faired well with men. My brother, sister, and I used to call her last husband Henry the VIII. His name was not Henry but Bud, but he was her eighth old man! Whether she had good luck or bad, I can only speculate. One thing was clear: good role models were difficult to find for either of my parents.

Both of my parents were only children; they both had significant deficits to overcome. Both came from neglectful and abusive backgrounds. Much of their experience history was thus carried into the next generation.

And The Two Shall Become... Two!

My parents met romantically at Palisades Gardens Roller Rink in San Diego, CA. They relate the story best as follows!

"We were skating around in circles (a picture of things to come), when the crowd faded from view. The attraction was most powerful; love at first sight. Within a few weeks we married." The Bible states if the blind shall lead the blind, will they both not fall into the ditch? My folks lived in the ditch! Neither had a realistic idea of how to be a spouse, let alone a parent, though as with most their intentions were for the best.

My father was looking for the all loving, all encouraging, all supportive mother/wife who would relieve his fears and provide him strength.

She was looking for the perfect father/husband, provider/protector who would always in kindness love her without reservation.

As with most couples, they attempted to redo or repair the wounds of their generations through their relationship. They lacked the skill and requisite maturity to accomplish this necessary task. No matter how hard they tried, they could never come to the realization of peace they desperately searched for.

Their dream was primarily fantasy. They lived for years on the brink of divorce, violence, poverty and separation, mixed with passionate love, uncanny loyalty, and uproarious laughter. When they were good, they were/are very good, and when there were bad, it was terrifying. Without the Lord at work in their lives, and ours, I am certain we would never have survived!

My dad had always been an under skilled, but hard worker. He was frequently unemployed, though he always found a way to provide for his family. His insecurity and poor coping skills made for an unstable home environment, as did my mom's frequent and severe illnesses and Irish temper.

Growing up in our family there was never a dull moment, though they were filled with anxiety and anger.

Many symptoms have developed in my brother, sister and me. These can be seen as "gifts" from our generational tree, and include:

1) Anger
2) Fear
3) Sexual Difficulties
4) Poverty
5) Cruelty
6) Depression
7) Drug Abuse
8) Divorce
9) Idolatry
10) Violence
11) Bitterness
12) Heart disease
13) Obesity
14) Diabetes
15) Mental Illness
16) Abuses
17) Alcoholism
18) Victimization (Powerlessness)
19) Occultism
20) Abandonment

There are probably others, but this list provides a fairly clear picture. Before proceeding further, there are two very important statements that must be made:

First, we are all responsible for our own sinful reactions. I cannot, nor do I blame my problems on anyone. I am merely using my family tree for an illustration, not vindication.

Second, most parents (including and especially mine) did the best they could considering their background, gifts and abilities. I am truly grateful for my parents, and would not trade them for any other.

A Simple Analysis

As with all symptoms, there is a much higher propensity of having the same problems occur in the present generation if they have been a part of previous generations. Even insurance companies are interested in your family history, and most physicians want to look back as far as your 3rd and 4th generation to determine what areas of preventative medicine to focus on.

People live what they observe. The traits my mom and dad learned were a composite of their families of origin. I brought my own identity difficulties, obsessions, compulsions, behavioral and effectual problems into my marriage (which my wife and children have graciously endured). Thank God for His grace and mercy for a loving and forgiving family.

The dynamics of my family created in me an unconscious compulsion to achieve and overcome, with a tremendous and insidious ability to sabotage my own growth in Christ. James was so right when he stated we are led away when enticed by our own lusts (desires).

> *"But every man is tempted, when he is drawn away of his own lust, and enticed."* (James 1:14)

How often I cried out to God for deliverance and healing. For years I could not understand why I was so vulnerable to Satanic attack in some areas, and so strong to overcome in others. My search through the scriptures has led me to a fuller, growing understanding of the causality and deliverance from the "sins of the father" (or previous generations).

This gives a basic picture of the natural. Every family tree is a little different. Every individual can suffer from different symptoms based upon their family of origin. Not everyone is going to be exactly the same. In many cases we see that these symptoms will skip generations.

Though the natural view may provide some of the information as to how symptoms or problems are passed down generationally, the view would not be complete without the spiritual/Biblical side. It is important to understand just how generational patterns occur, and exactly how to deal with them from a Biblical and psychological perspective.

However, first, an illustration would be helpful to demonstrate how the seed of the family tree continued, implanted deep in my heart, and which set in motion destructive consequences for my generation.

The White Picket Fence

It was a hot August morning, and my dad had asked me to paint our white picket fence. Just like most eight year olds do, I saw my dad as a hero. I would do anything to prove myself worthy of his affection; for him to be proud of me was my highest desire. I thought I could demonstrate my worth by painting the fence... just for him!

I vividly remember putting on my old clothes (which is somewhat redundant - since we were poor, all my clothes were old), gathered the paint and brush, and set out to transform our old picket fence into a beautiful showpiece. In truth, I got nearly as much paint on my clothes and the grass as on the fence (Eight year olds are not usually the most skilled at such things).

About halfway through the day, my mom brought me some finger sandwiches and Kool-aid (like she did for my dad). This seemed like an extra special touch for what was shaping up to be a most excellent day.

About 5:00 PM, I started cleaning the paint brushes and putting away the supplies in anticipation of my dad's arrival home. After tidying up, I sat down on my front porch, like a little Buddha, waiting for dad's arrival.

A few minutes later, my dad drove up, pulling his old but faithful car into the vacant lot next to our old house. After inspecting the rocks (a daily ritual, to make sure that new ones had not grown or been thrown at the house), he walked towards the house.

There I sat with positive expectations. He came through the front gate, walking past me without any acknowledgment (a fairly common routine). My heart beat a bit faster, knowing that after work my dad would typically enter the house, pat my mom on the head, kiss the dog, and change his clothes. Honest! How my mom could tolerate playing second fiddle to the dog, I'll never know!

After changing, my dad came back outside, again without seeming to notice me, and began to inspect the fence. My heart really began to beat faster. At times, my dad could be quite angry, and I had hopes today would not be one of those days.

As my dad began to approach the front of the house, I heard him speaking to himself. He was mumbling loud enough for me to hear some comments that would impact the course of my life for many years to come. He declared, "If you're going to do a man's job, you need a man to do it. Stan, you're never going to amount to (Expletives)!" POW!

At the very moment of his prophetic pronouncement, several things occurred in my heart. These prophetic utterances must be understood if we are to break the cycle of the iniquity of the fathers, and be equipped to bring about the restoration of the soul, the repairing of the breach (Isaiah 58: 12).

In the following figures, I have given an illustration of what occurred in the millisecond of time while I sat on that porch so many years ago. Let me describe it here; keep your heart open, since this pattern is typical of so many of God's wounded soldiers.

God created us with an incredible ability to survive. The word that my father spoke, and the look on his face, was instantaneously perceived through my ears, my eyes and my spirit as a statement of overwhelming danger. This was not the first time my dad had stated such things (we jokingly talk about it now as my dad's ability to speak "Navy"). But this was the time it "stuck."

Figure 2

I'LL SHOW YOU HOW GOOD I AM!

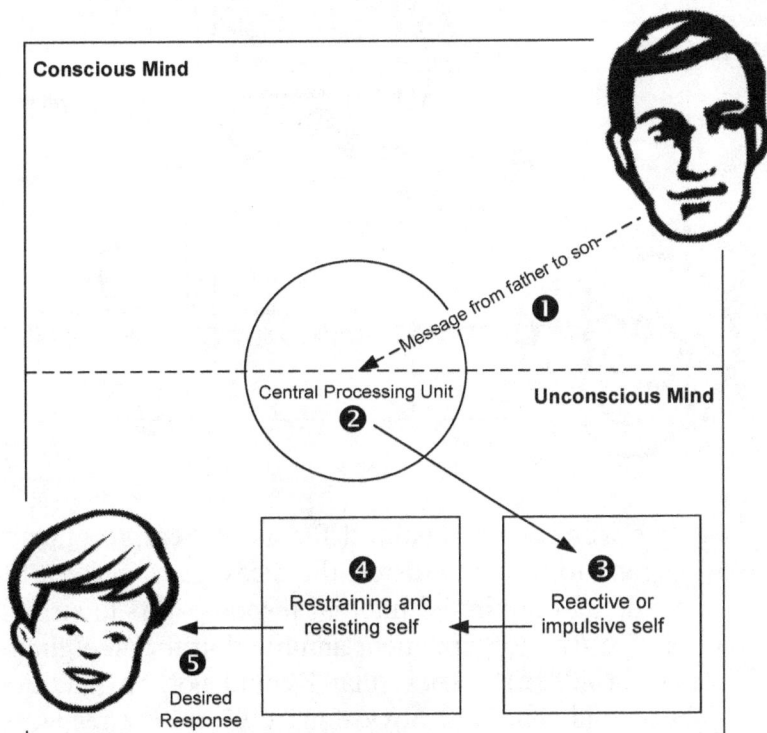

Figure 3

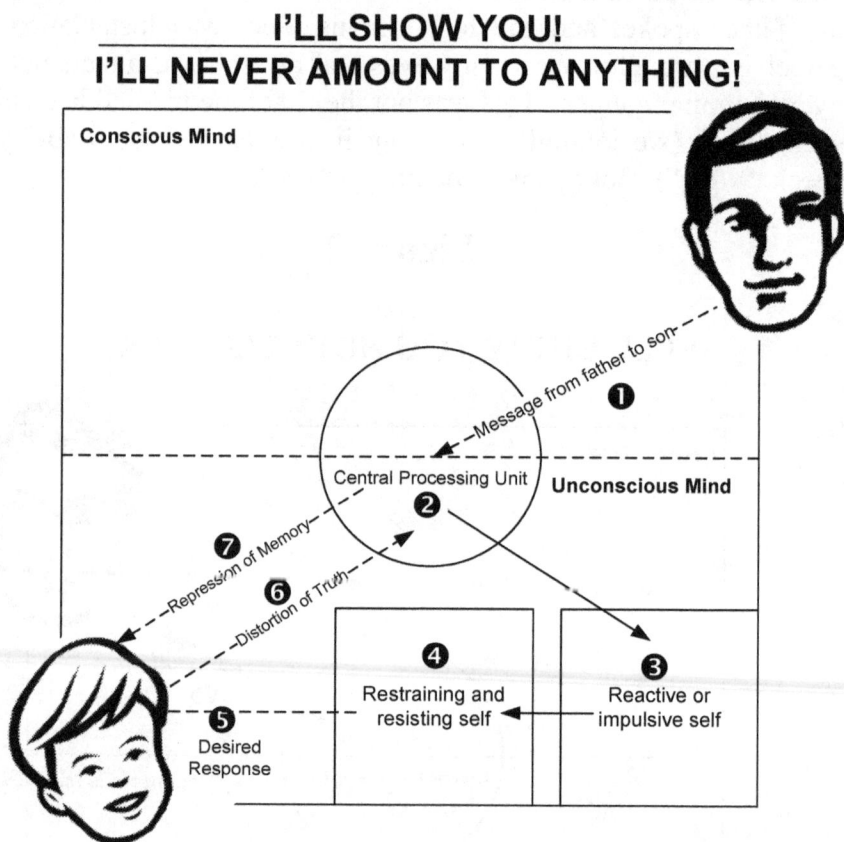

I'LL SHOW YOU!
I'LL NEVER AMOUNT TO ANYTHING!

Because this word was too painful for me to bear, too horrifying to face or respond to, I had to distort the message to make it tolerable. In essence, though my initial internal response was to strike back at my dad (a sure way to permanent annihilation for an eight year old, and totally forbidden), I knew that I could not. In addition I had always been told that "big boys don't cry" so my responses were limited at best.

The only way I could defend myself from this painful word was to change or twist (iniquity) the truth of the message, giving it a different meaning. Unconsciously, I re-routed the message, telling myself "he had a bad day" and "he didn't really mean it" and "I never liked painting anyway" and "it doesn't matter," etc.

I distorted the message, replacing the truth with a lie to survive. Further, I buried this memory out of consciousness. The result was a wounding of my soul that drove me compulsively towards a conflicting conclusion. Before discussing the results of this prophetic curse (puncture, pierce, malign), I must advance the story several years.

This memory was buried for a long, long time. As I mentioned earlier, at 12 I became a Christian, and fairly consistently applied myself to living the Christian life. Through a number of circumstances, unquestionably directed by the Lord, God revealed the stronghold (one of many that had to be torn down) that had brought me into bondage and kept me isolated from my natural father and my spiritual father.

Ben's Bonanza

Ben, who was 13 "going on 8" (one of several foster sons my wife, Karen, and I cared for in our home) had lived with us for about a year. I was working for a Christian-owned treatment center for troubled children as a counselor/director. One very hot August day, I asked him to paint the red wood fence in the back of our house.

As I drove to work that day, I began to become noticeably agitated. Though the day was quite uneventful, my agitation increased until "Navy" language began to manifest itself in my mind. Thoughts of Ben and the fence created images of revenge and retribution if he failed to meet my expectations. I could not understand why I was so agitated, though the Holy Spirit certainly knew. You see, just before this incident, I had made the mistake of asking the Lord for something I was not really ready to face...

The "Mistake"

Just prior to this memory returning, I had prayed a very specific and sincere prayer to the Lord. I had prayed, "Father, if there is anything in my heart, hurts from the past, unforgiveness that I am unconsciously harboring against anyone, please reveal it to me that I might be set free."

My spiritual walk had grown stale. I knew something had to change. This prayer, honored by the Lord, set in motion the necessary cleansing and rebuilding of my character that I needed (even though "I" didn't really think I needed it (pride, self-reliance, etc.).

As I drove up to the house, my "Navy" thoughts began to manifest. I got out of my old but reliable truck, walked through the door, through the house and out the back door.

Fortunately for my wife (and my own preservation), we had no rocks to inspect or dog in the house to kiss! I began to inspect the fence.

Also, of great fortune to Ben's well being, he was visiting a friend.

The fence had been painted fairly well, but it was far from perfect. Of course, it wouldn't have mattered how perfect it was. This was a time of reckoning for me, though I still had no recollection of my previous experience.

After inspecting the fence, I entered the house, ranting about what a worthless waste of human flesh my foster son was, and how I would teach him a lesson. I even ranted at Karen for not supervising him well enough.

Well, my wife was fairly meek and quiet, but with the boldness of the Lord she commanded "go to your room!" So I did. I had a small office off the dining area that was a private study.

Upon arriving in my "secret place," I cried out to the Lord. In the quiet of that place, God brought back to me the memory of the white picket fence. My weeping, anger, fear, hurt, etc. was immense. I had not cried like that in a long time.

As I experienced the emotion connected with the memory that had been buried for so long, I cried out to God for His forgiveness for having held a root of bitterness in my heart.

I sought His cleansing through repentance. This was the beginning of my process of reconciliation with my father. Not only did I have to repent before the Lord, but I had to face my dad. Not to condemn and judge, but to forgive, seek forgiveness, place responsibility (his - thoughtless statements and mine - unforgiveness and rejection of him), and seek reconciliation. This talk, filled with high anxiety, was the start of a relationship that is far from perfect, but is at least moving in the right direction (more on this later).

The Schism (or, The Two Headed Monster)

The impact of my dad's prophetic word was two-fold. I developed an internally diabolic way of thinking and acting. On one level, I determined in my heart I would prove to my dad that he was wrong. "How dare he," and "I'll show him," were primary themes!

I became a compulsive over achiever with obsessions for success, and fears of failure and abandonment. I became a sports-aholic, achievement-aholic, even a church-religious-aholic as I dove into one activity after another trying to win my dad's approval. Unfortunately, since my dad had never achieved any sense of approval himself from his mother and father, he did not have it to give. He always tried to give what he had, but the pitcher of approval he tried to pour from was empty.

I never did receive his attention and approval, but I continued the chase. I did achieve a modicum of success. Yet, try as I might, I could never overcome my sense of inadequacy and worthlessness.

My, how God was gracious in loving me during the paper chase for my Ph.D. I chased after education, success, even ministry, to satisfy the "hole in my soul." My desire for success was only superseded by a genuine desire to be healed, whole, and complete in Him (conformed to the image of Christ), and my ability to sabotage my own success.

There were many times when I came close to success, but I would make a mistake, sin, or in some other way sabotage myself. Though I desperately wanted to please and disprove the "prophetic curse," my inner self had secretly agreed with the message. In essence, I believed my dad"s report: "You'll never amount to anything."

In James 1:8 the writer states *"a double-minded man is unstable in all his ways."*

In Jeremiah 17:10 it states, *"the heart is deceitful above all things and desperately wicked."*

I believed the two-headed monster - the split thinking in mind and heart - completely (though unconsciously).

I was well aware of the Lord's promises to set me at liberty from sin and its results. The battle was already won on the cross, and had already been appropriated to me through the Holy Spirit by God's wonderful grace. Yet, no matter how I tried, the core inside of me believed I would never amount to anything in the eyes of the one whose opinion mattered most - my dad. I desperately needed and ultimately received (and am still growing in) God's deliverance and heart mending. This process will be discussed in the remainder of this book.

All happy families resemble one another; every unhappy family is unhappy in its own way.

- Leo Tolstoy -

Stan E. DeKoven, Ph.D.

Chapter Three

The Genesis - After its Kind

Inherent in the Genesis account (Genesis 1:21-31) is an important teaching. When God created the birds, mammals, and especially mankind, He enabled them to reproduce (be fruitful and multiply) after their own kind. Within the seed pod in plants, animals and man is the creative potential of life. When a seed is planted, when sperm and egg unite, the result will be (barring a tragic mutation) the development of a plant or person in the likeness of its parents. This is a universal principle.

When God created man, He did so in planting His own identity into us. That identity creates in us the desires for creation, pleasure, joy, love and family. Of course, as fallen humans we no longer carry the pure identity that Adam (mankind, including Adam and Eve) carried before the fall. Sin in our seed, from Adam to now, has marred the image of God in us. Due to sin, we are all vulnerable to the damage, pain and suffering from our forefathers.

In truth, we are a result of the "seed" that has been planted within us, both destructive through sin and productive through Christ.

The Results

The results in my family of origin and those of most people in our world are varied. Ultimately, we have all experienced a certain amount of brokenness. The results of brokenness can include insecurity, jealousy, betrayal, guilt, shame, bitterness and compulsiveness. Each is significant.

Insecurity

Both men and women receive our primary sense of self from the father. Our identities, including a good or bad image of ourselves, are developed in the interactions between the father and son (or daughter). This includes our sexual identity or our primary "maleness" and "femaleness."

When the father is absent, distant or abusive, an underlying sense of insecurity can develop. Even when the father is present and active in a home, his influence is lessened by the degree of dysfunction he carries from his family of origin.

Jealousy

Rivalry for affection and attention was pronounced in our family. My fear of "never amounting to anything" made me suspicious of anyone who was successful, happy, and productive.

Comparisons with everyone else to determine my credibility or merit became an obsession.

Fantasies of being the victor over all opponents became the norm. Thus, my ability to achieve close and intimate friends and confidants was impaired. And the plot thickens.

Betrayal

Betrayal of one's trust in authority, parents, friends, etc., creates hostility, often preceding rejection by others. One develops an anticipation of betrayal, and usually acts in a non-trusting manner to "test" the trustworthiness of another. Even if they "pass" the test, it does not matter, since an individual can not believe that the trust was real. Dr. Earle Fox in his book *Biblical Inner Healing* emphasizes that this is caused by a rupture in the faith/dependency relationship of early childhood. That is, as children we put our entire trust in caregivers who are unable (because of the fall and sin) to meet our primary trust needs. Thus a rupture occurs or a wounding of the soul, which sets in motion this deep and pervasive sense of betrayal and fear of the same.

Unaware of the personal sabotage, people either choose obviously untrustworthy individuals to associate with, or systematically set up rejection and betrayal through their own untrustworthy acts. Around and around the cycle goes, and where it stops nobody can know.

Guilt and Shame

Guilt is always easier to manage than shame. Guilt is an action of one's consciousness when a moral code has been violated. Forgiveness and repentance (when needed) will satisfy healthy guilt.

However, with shame, almost nothing seems to satisfy. Ownership of unworthiness as an inherited or acquired trait traps the individual in a circular belief. The flawed belief goes something like this: "I am internally flawed. Thus, all that I do, all that I am, and all I will ever be is flawed. Shame on me. Woe is me." Isaiah, the prophet, stated a fact that he was a man of unclean lips (Isaiah 6:5). For him, there was the burning coal from off the altar that took away his iniquity.

Those with shame-based self-perceptions of unworthiness can never find a fire hot enough to burn away the mark of the scarred. To a child, good things happen to good people, and bad things happen to bad people. "With all the bad, we must have somehow earned our lot," they think. "We are bad in spite of copious evidence to the contrary."

Bitterness

For most of my upbringing, I was too compulsive and angry to even see my bitterness. A bitter root in the heart of a person will sour all aspects of his/her personality.

For me, bitterness would exude from me in sarcastic comments (all in good fun, of course!) at the expense of others. After years of justification, one no longer can see the bitterness, but only the compensation -- wit, whimsy, sarcasm, criticism. Of course, the root had to go.

Compulsiveness

Insecurity creates a hunger and thirst without the ability to fulfill it. Our spiritual hunger and thirst are satisfied by drinking of the Living Water. Our spirit, which is under the Holy Spirit's control, is fully alive and able to receive wholeness from the beginning of salvation.

However, due to damage in the soul, the ability to "drink" from the fountain of life and "eat" of the flesh of His word is limited by the strongholds and wounds of the past.

Delusions/Wickedness

Lies can become entrenched in our minds until they feel like truth. Wickedness (often described as a dysfunctional lifestyle) can develop. All of these were a part of my heritage, passed on by my family tree. I struggled with many other difficult areas without knowledge of the source, or the power for deliverance or healing.

As members of the human race, we inherit traits from our families of origin. We are destined to repeat the patterns, beginning as seeds from our fathers to us, since the creative potential of our generations reside within us. To a great extent, we will produce as our parents produced, seed after its own kind. The results can be seen in our daily walk.

The Three Headed Monster

I have said to many of my clients, "Everyone has something to overcome. It is through our battles, our suffering, and our wilderness journey that we mature in Christ."

During a ministry trip to Eastern Europe, the Lord brought back to me a principle I intellectually knew but had never "known" its full meaning and impact. I was on a prayer walk when the revelation of the three pronged strategy of Satan was made clear. I could finally recognize why I walked so closely at times to the abyss of self-destruction, and how the Lord had protected me. It is not the details of my personal struggle that matters. God's plan and strategy to overcome are paramount.

> *"Do not love the world or anything in the world. If anyone loves the world, the love of the Father is not in him. For everything in the world-the cravings of sinful man, the lust of his eyes and the boasting of what he has and does - comes not from the Father but from the world. The world and its desires pass away, but the man who does the will of God lives forever."* (John 2:15-17)

Jesus encountered the same three-pronged attack in His wilderness experience with the devil, recorded in Luke 4: 1-13,

> *"And Jesus being full of the Holy Ghost returned from Jordan, and was led by the Spirit into the wilderness, Being forty days tempted of the devil. And in those days he did eat nothing: and when they were ended, he afterward hungered. And the devil said unto him, If thou be the Son of God, command this stone that it be made bread. And Jesus answered him, saying, It is written, That man shall not live by bread alone, but by every word of God. And the devil, taking him up into an high mountain, showed unto him all the kingdoms of the world in a moment of time. And the devil said unto him, All this power will I give thee, and the glory of them: for that is delivered unto me; and to whomsoever I will I give it. If thou therefore wilt worship me, all shall be thine. And Jesus answered and said unto him, Get thee behind me, Satan: for it is written, Thou shalt worship the Lord thy*

God, and him only shalt thou serve. And he brought him to Jerusalem, and set him on a pinnacle of the temple, and said unto him, If thou be the Son of God, cast thyself down from hence: For it is written, He shall give his angels charge over thee, to keep thee: And in their hands they shall bear thee up, lest at any time thou dash thy foot against a stone. And Jesus answering said unto him, It is said, Thou shalt not tempt the Lord thy God. And when the devil had ended all the temptation, he departed from him for a season." (Luke 4:1-13)

This story is also reported in Matthew 4:1-11 and Mark 1:12-13. Jesus was tempted in areas of the flesh, the lust of the eyes and the pride (self-sufficiency outside of God) of life.

Christ defeated Satan in these areas of temptation, though we all fail at times. For those in recovery, especially those in ministry, Satan will often attack us with a three-pronged approach in an attempt to crush us. If he can exploit a wound caused by our own failure and sin, if he can hook us with self-condemnation, guilt and shame, he can immobilize us from flowing in the power of the Spirit as God intended. Even in our time of crushing, the Lord has dispatched His angels to assist us. In Matthew 4:11 we read *"Then the devil left Him, and angels came and attended him"*.

He promises forgiveness, and He will strengthen us in our weakness, no matter how we have failed God, ourselves or others. As we allow God's Word to heal us, we can walk in His will and fulfill our destiny.

The Trees of Life

In figures 4 & 5 (The Trees of Knowledge of Good and Evil) we have an illustrative picture of a most important concept. We must fully grasp all Christ has done for us through His death on the cross. In spite of our dysfunction, which is ultimately a result of inherited disobedience (through Satan), the cross of Christ, when applied to our heart, is more than powerful enough to eradicate sin and its results. Ultimately, we must all die just as a seed does if we are to have Christ's life flows through us.

In the illustration, there are two trees that come from two seeds. The main tree (a/b) is the tree of our individual life, which comes from the natural seed of mom and dad, and carries the genetic imprint of generations past. This is the tree of knowledge of good and evil. Through that seed our natural temperament forms, which is molded or impacted by our environment, forming our character or personality.

Tree (b) is the tree of knowledge of good and evil (Genesis 2:15-17), which was and is eaten in disobedience, and creates in us as individuals the seed of rebellion and the root of every form of evil.

The third tree, the tree of life (c) (Genesis 2:9) is the Christ whom we partake of at the time of salvation, and which brings life to all who receive.

As the pictures illustrate, the tree which is our life, even as Christians, can continue to bear fruit that we do not want it to bear. That is, our symptoms, whether behavioral or emotional, continue to live until the axe is laid to the root of our old carnal nature. The axe is the two-edged sword, the Word of God, and when applied to our root system as led by the Holy Spirit, cuts off the old from the source of supply. As we abide in the vine and partake of Christ, we are renewed, refreshed, restored and reconciled daily.

This is a process more than an event! It begins, and continues until Christ is fully formed within us.

> *"My dear children, for whom I am again in the pains of childbirth until Christ is formed in you"* (Galatians 4:19).

At that time we will no longer bear the old fruit, but will instead see the old fruit die for lack of nurturing. The fruit of the Spirit will grow because of our faithful feasting on the Word as our worship.

As believers, we have the choice to eat of the tree of life or the tree of the knowledge of good and evil; to dwell under the shadow of the Almighty's wing or wing it on our own. Many have been ignorant of the effects of the tree leading to death and do not understand how we have inherited our present better symptomatic pattern.

Another Joe

Joe was a 29 year old carpenter from a nearby city, who was referred for counseling by his pastor. His pastor had been counseling Joe's wife regarding how she might handle more effectively Joe's explosive anger, threatening behavior and extremely low self-esteem.

As with most clients, Joe was somewhat apprehensive about the process of "spilling his guts" to a stranger. However, after an initial testing period, he began to share about his unique yet familiar story.

Joe was the eldest child in a family of three, and the only son. His father left home when Joe was 8, under unclear and undisclosed circumstances. His father's disappearance is one of the many things which were never discussed in his home. Joe did have a step father, but he was never accepted as any more than the bread winner. It was made clear from the start that he was to have nothing to do with the disciple of the children and was marginalized in terms of influence.

Joe had been in therapy before, but had made little progress. The discussion had been around the loss of his father which Joe saw as a minor event. In truth, and as is often the case, he was not ready to deal with the ramifications of the loss with the first counselor. He did nave many unresolved issues with his mother, but the father issues were predominant.

Joe began to share more openly about the sense of loss he had in relation to his father. As with most boys and girls of age 8, he interjected the loss, developing a belief that he had caused his father to leave. He also had a very strong fear that the same thing would also happen to him (that is, secretly he blamed his mother for driving his father away which was not true, and keeping his step-dad from bonding with him, which was partially true), that his wife would "drive his away" or he would lose her. Of course, the expectation moved him to unconsciously behave in a way to create the situation where his self fulfilling prophecy would come to pass.

After a few weeks of counseling, Joe began to gain insight and a better handle on his behavior. We began to develop some new strategies for dealing with his feelings and meetings his extreme dependency needs in a more appropriate ways. This made a positive impact, but there were still issues that we could not discover through stand talk therapy. There seemed to be forces beyond his personal history that continued to drive him to fits of anger, depression and despair. There was a deeper ministry needed, which occurred as we looked fully into the depths of his generational patterns. More on this later.

To strengthen our scriptural position, it is important to explain more fully biblical patterns, as examples of God's plan for our full deliverance.

Figure 4

Longsuffering

Temperance   Goodness

Faith   Love   Peace

Meakness   Gentleness

Joy

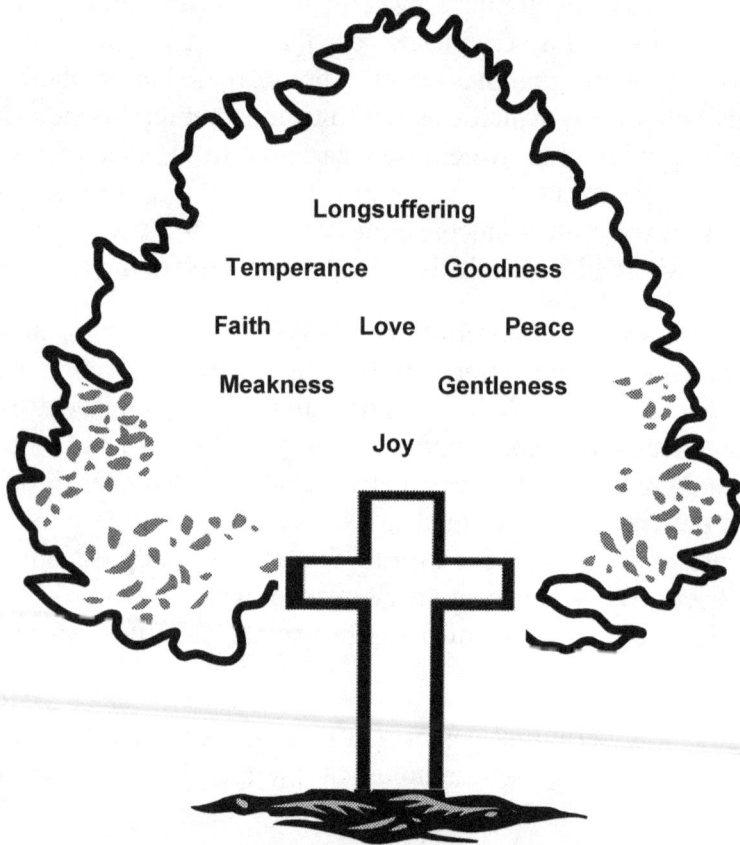

Tree of Life (Christ)

The cross applied to one's life will overshadow the deeds of the flesh and produce the fruit of the Spirit which is sanctification. See Galatians 5:22, "…the fruit of the spirit is…"

Figure 5

Psychological Symptoms

Depression   Low Self-Worth

Sexual Sin

Anger   Anxiety

False Worship

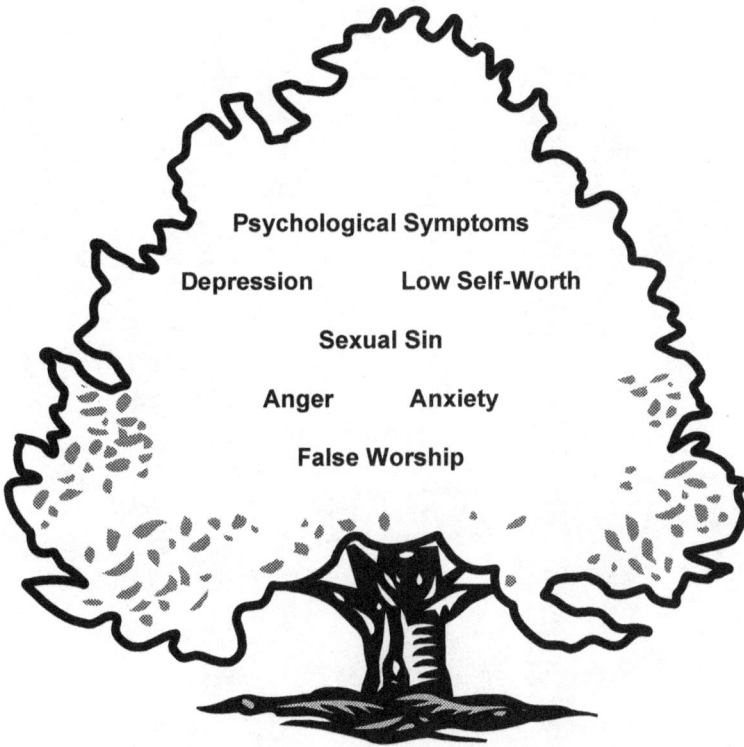

The Roots of Iniquity

Anger, Fear   Idolatry, Hatred*

Immorality   Lack of Human Love

Lack of Affirmation   Betrayal, Bitterness

Abuse, Rebellion   Unforgiveness

* The behaviors that bring a curse: Deut. 5:9; 27:15-26; 28:15, Isa. 31:2, Jer. 31:30 Acts 8:23 Jam. 3:6

The most important thing a father can do for his children is to love their mother.

- Theodore Hesburgh

Chapter Four

The Biblical Pattern: The Exodus

In Exodus 20, beginning with verse one, it reads,

> *"And God spoke all these words: "I am the Lord your God who brought you out of the land of Egypt, out of the house of slavery. You shall have no other gods before me. You shall not make for yourself an idol or any likeness of what is in Heaven above, or on the Earth beneath, or in the water under the Earth. You shall not worship them or serve them; for I the Lord your God am a jealous God, visiting the iniquity of the fathers on the children on the 3rd and 4th generations of those who hate me, but showing loving kindness to thousands who love me and keep my commandments."*

When I first read this passage of scripture, and the parallel passages in Exodus 34, Numbers 14, and elsewhere in the Bible, it troubled me. I received a sense of hopelessness and despair, thinking there would be no help for someone such as me.

There is no question my great grandfather, my grandfather, and even my father (up until the time that he was born-again) had a hatred or at least a disregard for the laws, plans, and principles of God.

Yet, I realized that in Christ, as the scripture says in 2 Corinthians 5:17, Therefore if any man *be* in Christ, *he* is an new creature: old things are passed away, behold all things are become new.

As a new creation, I was free from the penalty of my sin. However, as I have come to realize through experience and study, the story does not end there. There remained the pattern of iniquity that had to be eradicated from my life. This iniquity, which from the Hebrew is the word "*avon*", comes from the root word "avah" meaning to bend or distort. Iniquity then is by definition the propensity towards sin (especially a certain type or category of sin), or the twisting of our character due to sin.

The results of disobedience to the laws of God are the curse of the iniquities of the fathers being visited through a spiritual dynamic which must be dealt with through the Word of God.

We must affirm that indeed Jesus was "bruised for our iniquities" and our iniquities were laid on him. (Isaiah 53:5-6) Further, in Galatians 3:13, we see that Jesus became the curse for us.

> *"Christ redeemed us from the curse of the law by becoming a curse for us, for it is written: 'Cursed is everyone who is hung on a tree.'"*

The Lord Jesus Christ, though His death and resurrection has made complete provision for all of us. He became a curse for us by being crucified on the cross for our sins.

However, the patterns people learn continue even after our born again experience! Iniquity or behavioral patterns often remain, and can originate through demonic activity, such as idolatry or witchcraft, unconfessed sins, or genetically through physical weakness and sickness, creating a susceptibility and predisposition for certain diseases. Further, emotional and psychological disorders, personality tendencies or mental conflict can affect us[3].

---

[3] For more on this important subject, the author would refer you to the outstanding study by Dr. Doug Jarrard (see the bibliography in the back of this book).

What has been taught to us in the past, what we have seen and observed through the modeling process can affect us in the present. Though our spirit is made whole through salvation in Christ, the transformation of our soul and the cleansing of our iniquities must occur for true freedom in Christ to be our daily experience.

Our personal responsibility for sin, the sins of our past generations, has been broken by the blood of Jesus. I cannot confess my father's, grandfather's or my great-grandfather's sins. I cannot repent for them to receive cleansing for them and their sins. I can only receive forgiveness for myself by the blood of Jesus. As I confess my sin before Him, I receive the Lord Jesus Christ and the Holy Spirit resides within me.

Problems **can** be passed on from generation to generation. Certain propensities toward sin, sickness, and toward personality patterns are transmitted from generation to generation. What must be discovered is how these problems are transmitted, not just in the natural, but through the spiritual realm. To truly recover and become all that God wants us to be, we must deal with all aspects of how we developed the symptoms and difficulties that we presently face.

It is not enough just to work through the unforgiveness or resentment that may occur because of inadequate parenting. It is not enough just to recognize our physiological difficulties and establish, for instance, better eating habits, although those things are good. We must recognize that all of these problems have a root spiritual dynamic which can be discovered within the Word of God! Once discovered and acted upon, deliverance, healing and restoration become our full and rightful inheritance.

Our Father Abraham: Pattern of Deception

Abraham is the father of our faith, an example of all believers of obedience to the Lord. All Christians have been grafted into this great family, and we are co-inheritors of the grace of God through Christ. However, this is not the only "inheritance" that was transferred like spiritual DNA as we will see in the life of Abraham, Isaac, Jacob and Joseph.

Abraham, the man, was susceptible to temptation, and subject to weakness as any man. The Word of God does not hide his (or anyone's) weakness, but reveals them as patterns of understanding for us. As with Ahab (our next character example), in Abraham's life we see the pattern of destruction or iniquity, transferred generationally.

Abraham's Treachery

As with a large majority of men, Abraham was concerned about his own safety, and was not beyond self-protective interest even at the risk of his own wife.

> *"Now Abraham journeyed from there toward the land of the Negev, and settled between Kadesh and Shur; then he sojourned in Gerar. And Abraham said of Sarah his wife, 'She is my sister.' So Abimelech king of Gerar sent and took Sarah. But God came to Abimelech in a dream of the night, and said to him, 'Behold, you are a dead man because of the woman whom you have taken, for she is married.' Now Abimelech had not come near her; and he said, 'Lord, wilt Thou slay a nation, even though blameless?' 'Did he not himself say to me, 'She is my sister'? And she herself said, 'He is my brother.' In the integrity of my heart and the innocence of my hands I have done this.' Then God said to him in the dream, 'Yes, I know that in the integrity of your heart you have done this, and I also kept you from sinning against Me; therefore I did not let you touch her.' 'Now therefore, restore the man's wife, for he is a prophet, and he will pray for you, and you will live. But if you do not restore*

her, know that you shall surely die, you and all who are yours.' So Abimelech arose early in the morning and called all his servants and told all these things in their hearing; and the men were greatly frightened. Then Abimelech called Abraham and said to him, 'What have you done to us? And how have I sinned against you that you have brought on me and on my kingdom a great sin? You have done to me things that ought not to be done.' And Abimelech said to Abraham, 'What have you encountered, that you have done this thing.' And Abraham said, 'Because I thought, surely there is no fear of God in this place; and they will kill me because of my wife. Besides, she actually is my sister, the daughter of my father, but not the daughter of my mother, and she became my wife; and it came about, when God caused me to wander from my father's house, that I said to her, 'This is the kindness which you will show to me: everywhere we go, say of me, 'He is my brother.''' Abimelech then took sheep and oxen and male and female servants, and gave them to Abraham, and restored his wife Sarah to him. And Abimelech said, 'Behold, my land is before you; settle wherever you please.' And to Sarah he said, 'Behold, I have given your brother a thousand pieces of silver; behold, it is your vindication before all who are with you, and before all men you are cleared.' And Abraham prayed to God; and God healed Abimelech and his wife and his maids, so that they bore children. For the LORD had closed fast all the wombs of the household of Abimelech because of Sarah, Abraham's wife. " (Genesis 20:1-18)

Out of fear, Abraham was willing to lie and sacrifice his wife (also is half-sister). This deception was done <u>before</u> the birth of Isaac, the son of promise, yet the pattern of deception (iniquity) can be seen in the next generation.

Isaac – Like Father Like Son

Many years later, Abraham is dead, and Isaac and Rebekah had their twin sons, Esau and Jacob. Isaac had received the promise from God as had been given to his father, a promise of vast prosperity and eternal blessing. Almost immediately, in the same city as the previous incident, the flawed character is revealed;

> "So Isaac lived in Gerar. When the men of the place asked about his wife, he said, "She is my sister,' for he was afraid to say, 'my wife,' thinking, 'the men of the place might kill me on account of Rebekah, for she is beautiful.' And it came about, when he had been there a long time, that Abimelech king of the Philistines looked out through a window, and saw, and behold, Isaac was caressing his wife Rebekah. Then Abimelech called Isaac and said, 'Behold, certainly she is your wife! How then did you say, 'She is my sister'? And Isaac said to him, "Because I said, 'Lest I die on account of her.' And Abimelech said, 'What is this you have done to us? One of the people might easily have lain with your wife, and you would have brought guilt upon us.' So Abimelech charged all the people, saying, 'He who touches this man or his wife shall surely be put to death.' Now Isaac sowed in that land, and reaped in the same year a hundredfold. And the LORD blessed him." (Genesis 26:6-12).

As though an automatic process, the same deception or manipulation is acted out. The results could have been disastrous. The Iniquity of the fathers (generations) continues.

Jacob – the Master Manipulator

We advance our story, moving to the next generation, where we see Jacob (his name actually means manipulator), the prize of Rebekah, taking this spirit of deception or manipulation to new heights.

"Now it came about when Isaac was old..." (Gen. 27:1a).

The 27th chapter of Genesis continues to describe a joint venture to deceive Isaac (reaping what was sown) and manipulating the blessing of Esau to Jacob. This was accomplished, setting in motion a life of wandering for Jacob, who became a master manipulator. Though he also received the promise of inheritance and blessing from God, his deceptive, usurping manipulative character (iniquity, perverse or twisted perception of truth) always had a plan "B" until finally apprehended by God.

All Dressed Up and Nowhere To Go

In the 31st chapter of Genesis, God speaks to Jacob, instructing him to return to his homeland (v3). Jacob, seeing that it would be to his advantage to obey God (due to Laban's change of attitude towards his son-in-law) prepares for his return. Of course, Jacob is justifiably concerned about facing his brother Esau, assuming his brother's vow to kill him was still intact. This is Jacob's inimitable style, he sets things up so he can escape if needed. He divides the women and children, livestock and other material goods, into two camps, and sends them ahead of him to encounter Esau. What a man of character.

In the 24th verse of the 32 chapter, a most interesting thing occurs. Jacob, having set in motion his plan "B" hoping to save his neck and manipulate favor with Esau, was left all alone. He had none of the emotional or physical props to support himself, and when all if these helps vanished, he was forced to encounter God.

> *"Then Jacob was left alone, and a man wrestled with him until daybreak. And when he saw that he had not prevailed against him, he touched the socket of his thigh; so the socket of Jacob's thigh was dislocated while he wrestled with him. Then he said, 'Let me go, for the dawn*

is breaking.' But he said, 'I will not let you go unless you bless me.' So he said to him, 'What is your name?' And he said, 'Jacob.' And he said, 'Your name shall no longer be Jacob, but Israel; for you have striven with God and with men and have prevailed.' Then Jacob asked him and said, 'Please tell me your name.' But he said, 'Why is it that you ask my name?' And he blessed him there. So Jacob named the place Peniel, for he said, 'I have seen God face to face, yet my life has been preserved.' Now the sun rose upon him just as he crossed over Penuel, and he was limping on his thigh. Therefore, to this day the sons of Israel do not eat the sinew of the hip which is on the socket of the thigh, because he touched the socket of Jacob's thigh in the sinew of the hip."

In this encounter we see several important things. First Jacob was truly alone, and in a place of vulnerability. This is often needed for us to receive from the Lord. When it states that he wrestled with God it means that he held on for dear life. At any moment, as demonstrated by the dislocation of Jacob's hip by a simple touch, God (theophany) could have destroyed him if he desired to do so. Yet, Jacob, as with many of us, in his ignorance, still asks for a blessing, or if you will, payment from God for his troubles. As was his nature, the deceptive thread of iniquity was pervasive, and his desire was to receive something for himself.

The Lord does not respond directly to Jacob's request, but instead confronts him with a profound question, "What is your name?" (Vs 27). Of course, the Lord new his name. However, Jacob was, in this moment of exhaustion from the struggle with God, confronted with who he really was. The Lord stating to him, what is your identity, who are you really? His only response was "I am (or my identity is) Jacob (usurper, manipulator).

Apparently Jacob's response was without his usual guile. The honesty of his response, though still hidden somewhat from Jacob (see Vs 29) opened the door of his heart to receive a word of transforming power; *"your name* (identity) *will no longer be Jacob* (manipulator) *but Israel* (Prince of God)"

The Lord did bless Jacob. (Vs 29) Though there continued to be significant problems in Jacob/Israel's household, this power encounter began the transformation process that lead to the eradication of the generational curse of pattern of iniquity.

Joseph's Journey

If the fourth generation form Abraham's deception, Joseph, sold into slavery (deceiving Jacob, reaping what was sown) has ample opportunity to continue the pattern of iniquity. However, Joseph, who is a type of Christ, lived in perfect obedience, and refused to lie for his own protection. In turn he became a provider for his entire family. Thus through obedience to God and diligence to serve Potipher and Pharaoh, the generational curse or pattern was broken, and the blessings began to flow for the next several generations.

Ahab's Abyss

One of the clearest Biblical pictures of generational iniquity is seen in the family tree of Ahab. I've always been fascinated with the various kings and how, in spite of their position of power and influence, they could stray away so diabolically from the truths of God's Word.

Ahab was certainly an interesting character. When reviewing the scriptural evidence of not only Ahab's problems, but the difficulties found within the entire family tree of Ahab, we see specific patterns or types of how patterns are developed.

Ornery Omri

> *"But Omri did evil in the eyes of the LORD and sinned more than all those before him. He walked in all the ways of Jeroboam son of Nebat and in his sin, which he had caused Israel to commit, so that hey provoked the LORD, the God of Israel, to anger by their worthless idols. As for the other events of Omri's reign, what he did and the things he achieved, are they nit written in the book of the annals of the kings of Israel?"* (I Kings 16:25-28).

Omri rested with his fathers and was buried in Samaria. And Ahab his son succeeded him as king.

The story of Ahab actually begins with his father, Omri, a most wicked king in Israel; I call him Omri the ornery. Omri was quite rebellious, and raising up idols within Israel against the laws of God.

Omri had a little boy named Ahab. As a king's son, Ahab was raised in the palace with perfect access to his father, able to observe all his father and mother did. He was taught by the environmental pattern, the modeling process. The various spiritually correct and incorrect behavioral patterns that Omri did, Ahab observed.

> *"(There was never a man like Ahab, who sold himself to do evil in the eyes of the LORD, urged on by Jezebel his wife. He behaved in the vilest manner by going after idols, like the Amorites the LORD drove out before Israel.) When Ahab heard these words, he tore his clothes, put on a sackcloth and fasted. Then the word of the LORD came to Elijah the Tishbite: 'Have you noticed how Ahab has humbled himself, I will not bring this disaster in his day, but I will bring it on his house in the days of his son,'"* (I Kings 21:25-29).

Ahab not only learned the tricks of his father, but he had increased them, literally selling himself to do evil! The Bible also indicates that Jezebel, his wife tended to incite and encourage him to do evil things. This couple was a match made in Hell!

From Ahab and Jezebel there were many sons and servants that were a part of the family tree. In II Kings 10: 7-10, we see the fulfillment of the promise that came through the lips of the prophet Elijah.

Even though this is a specific promise to a specific family, we can see it has meaning for us - even today.

> *"When the letter arrived, these men took the princes and slaughtered all seventy of them. They put their heads in baskets and sent them to Jehu in Jezreel. When the messenger arrived, he told Jehu, 'They have brought the heads of the princes.' Then Jehu ordered, 'Put them in two piles at the entrance of the city gate until morning.' The next morning Jehu went out. He stood before all the people and said, 'You are innocent. It was I who conspired against my master and killed him, but who killed all these? Know the, that not a word the LORD has spoken against the house of Ahab will fail. The LORD has done what he promised through his servant Elijah,'"* (II Kings 10:7-10).

This specific promise to wipe out the family tree of Ahab and Omri was fulfilled.

Fortunately for those of us in Christ, the curse placed upon us is removed.

> *"All of also lived among them at one time, gratifying the cravings of our sinful nature and following its desires and thoughts. Like the rest, we were by nature objects of wrath,"* (Ephesians 2:3).

The curse of the law has been lifted (Galatians 3:13)

Yet, many of the behavioral patterns continue from generation to generation; they do so because of spiritual forces that are behind the activities of man.

Blessings and Curses

Before we look in depth at the spiritual forces behind the transmission of family patterns, an understanding of the blessings and curses found in scripture for our proper or improper relationship with the Lord is needed.

In the book of Deuteronomy 27 and 28, one can produce a listing of the various blessings and curses appropriated by the people of God living in obedience or disobedience to the Lord. I would encourage you to read these chapters for a clearer understanding of their importance.

According to the scripture, there is a promise from the Lord that various curses will occur based upon the behaviors and attitudes that people have toward God and toward their fellow man. Derek Prince in his book, *Blessing or Curse: You Can Choose!* summarize for us the curses and blessings into the following categories:

Blessings	Curses
Exaltation	Humiliation (Shame)
Health	Barrenness, unfaithfulness
Reproductiveness	Mental and Physical Sickness
Prosperity	Family Breakdown
Victory	Poverty
God's Favor	Defeat, Oppression, Failure, God's disfavor

God's Word says we are to love the Lord our God with our heart, soul, mind and strength, and our neighbors as ourselves (Luke 10:27).

When we do so, we fulfill the entire law. Of course, none of us have completely followed those two principles perfectly. No one is able to. Before we knew Christ, we were unable to live a life of righteousness before our God. Thus our need for Christ.

When I look back at my family generational pattern, I see a number of the behaviors listed in Deuteronomy 27 that my family participated in. They include: Idolatry, dishonoring father and mother, violating people's boundaries, mistreating and leading people astray, taking from widows and orphans, sexual sins, misrepresentation in financial dealings.

Virtually all the behaviors that could bring a curse are a part of my family tree. Because of these sins, a curse was "visited"[4] upon my generational pattern. This occurred by our own hand, our own doings. Although the power and influence of the curse was broken when we came to know Christ, there is still a continuing reaping for those things that have been sown. Behaviorally, emotionally, environmentally, and even spiritually the results of iniquity is still manifested in families over time.

Along with the curses for disobedience come the wonderful blessings of God for obedience. It is appropriate to focus on the blessings, but we must look at them in proper balance. The blessings are for those who walk in perfect obedience!

Very few of us walk in absolute obedience to God's Word. In spite of our inadequacy, God has poured out His blessings upon us because of His grace and mercy. We are a blessed people, and He wants us to live in full accordance to the exceeding great and

---

[4] We do not know how this occurs specifically, though we know that God is the initiator of this process (see Ex 20:1-5).

precious promises He has given to us. That is, according to the blessings He has bestowed upon us in Christ Jesus. The covenant of Abraham has been provided to us as grafted in members of the House of God. (see Gal. 3:29 & Rom. 9).

Throughout Deuteronomy 28, the many blessings and curses are listed. To summarize, the Bible says we are cursed if we enter into idolatry, if we dishonor our parents, if we are cruel, if we live with lust and immorality, if we lack hospitality, if we mistreat our neighbors, are given to bribery and dishonest gain, if we do not keep the commandments of the Lord and hearken unto the voice of God.

That is quite a list, but there's more. We are cursed if we do not live according to the plans and precepts of God (Deuteronomy 15). These curses (or the results of disobedience) include barrenness, guilt, disease or infirmities, despair or disappointment, adversity of all different kinds, a lack of the ability to experience comfort, bondage, poverty, hard heartedness and powerlessness.

This is an overwhelming list. Sadly, as I read these, I could not help but compare them to people raised in dysfunctional families. Some of the characteristics of adult children of dysfunctional families are so very similar[5]. They include:

1. We become **isolated and afraid** of people and authority figures. **Angry people** and **personal criticism** frighten us. We either become dysfunctional ourselves or marry someone who is, or both. Failing that, we find a compulsive personality such as a workaholic, to fulfill our subconscious need for **abandonment**.

2. We view life as victims, and we are attracted to weakness in our love, friendship, and career relationships.

3. We have an overdeveloped sense of responsibility, and it is easy for us to be concerned with others rather than ourselves.

---

[5] See *Twelve Steps to Wholeness* by Dr. DeKoven.

This helps us to avoid looking too closely at our own faults, and to avoid responsibility for ourselves. Somehow we feel **guilty** if we stand up for ourselves instead of giving in to others.

4. We become **addicted** to excitement in all our affairs. We confuse love with pity, and we tend to rescue others and try to "fix" them.

5. We have denied feelings from our traumatic childhood and have lost the ability to express even comfortable feelings such as joy or happiness.

6. We judge others harshly and **fear** the judgment of others; yet we also criticize and judge others.

7. We are terrified of **abandonment** and will do almost anything to hold onto a relationship rather than experience the painful feeling of abandonment. We develop this from living in a compulsive environment where no one was emotionally "there" for us.

8. As all compulsions are a part of a family dysfunction, we took on the symptoms early in **childhood** and **carried them into adulthood**. Even though we may never act out compulsive behaviors.

Individuals who have come to know Christ and are living their life the best that they know how may still experience many of the same curses (symptoms) listed: shame and guilt, a sense of disappointment, despair, that sense of bondage, unable to experience peace and comfort, seemingly powerless to overcome.

According to the Word of God, these curses or behavioral patterns should no longer be part of a Christian's life. The Bible says in Romans 8:37:

> *"No, in all these things we are more than conquerors through him that loved us."*

He has promised us blessings and prosperity. Yet, I have found that so many Christians do not live according to their potential in God. The evidence is overwhelming that curses or symptoms are transmitted through our family trees from generation to generation, and must be fully dealt with by the power of God. This underlying spiritual truth has not been fully understood. It must become a revelation to us, so that with wisdom we will be able to become free of our present dysfunctional generational pattern.

Blessings and Cursing Defined

In a Trauma and Sexuality workshop held in San Diego, Betty Gazaway, a family counselor who ministers in generational healing, defined blessing and cursing in a unique way. I am grateful to her for permission to paraphrase her workshop information in this book.

Blessings can be transferred from the parent to the child (or other significant others) in four primary ways:

1. <u>Affirmation</u> of meaningful touch, through loving, appropriate hugs, kisses, and other forms of intimate closeness. This produces the fruit of security.

2. <u>Affirmation</u> of positive words that lead to a healthy self-concept of esteem. *"Likewise the tongue is a small part of the body, by it makes great boasts. Consider what a great forest is set on fire by a small spark,"* (James 3:5).

"The tongue also is a fire, a world of evil among the parts of the body. It corrupts the whole person, sets the whole course of his life on fire, and is itself set on fire by hell," (James 3:6).

"But the tongue can no man tame; it is an unruly evil, full of deadly poison," (James 3:8).

3. <u>Affirmation</u> from the expression of high value. Abraham laid hands on Isaac, Isaac on Jacob, Israel on his twelve, Moses on Joshua, and ultimately Jesus passed on to his disciples a prophecy of **high value or worth**. The uniqueness of their calling, mixed with the favor and blessing of the father (natural or spiritual), created a sense of worth for the recipient.

4. <u>Affirmation</u> of a special future. Along with the affirmation of high value or esteem came the blessing that the future was special, that they had a destiny to fulfill. This provides the **purpose** that releases creative and courageous behavior so needed in the body of Christ.

A Testimony

In a church that we pastored, we have a ritual celebration - a rite of passage. When our young men and women reach their twelfth birthday (or as soon as possible thereafter) we hold a special service for them. We have the child and parents read and discuss the scriptural references on blessings on fatherhood and parent/child responsibility. On the day of the service, the parents would be encouraged to pronounce a blessing on their child, followed by ministry to the child and parents. We also welcome them into the adult community, showing respect, honor and proclaim the affirmation listed here.

We see remarkable results from this blessing service (borrowed somewhat from the Jewish Bar Mitzvah), and dramatic changes as young men and women receive and embrace the Word of the Lord. This can also be a time of important family or even generational healing.

Every child needs blessings to develop a healthy and Godly identity. No one receives it fully, and where the blessings are missing, cursing can result.

Some of the Bible texts that support this are:

"The LORD bless you and keep you; the LORD make his face shine upon you and be gracious to you; the LORD turn his face toward you and give you peace. So they will put my name on the Israelites, and I will bless them," (Num. 6:24-27).

"Marry and have sons and daughters; find wives for you sons and give your daughters in marriage, so that they too may have sons and daughters. Increase in number there; do not decrease. Also, seek the peace and prosperity of the city to which I have carried you into exile. Pray to the LORD for it, because if it prospers, you too will prosper," (Jeremiah 29:6-27).

"For I know the plans I have for you,' declares the LORD, 'plans to prosper you and not to harm you, plans to give you hope and a future. Then you will call upon me and come and pray to me, and I will listen to you. You will seek me and find me when you seek me with all your heart. I will be found by you,' declares the LORD, ' and will bring you back from captivity. I will gather you from all the nations and places where I have banished you,' declares the LORD, ' and will bring you back to the place from which I carried you into exile.' You may say, 'The LORD has raised up prophets for us in Babylon,'" (Jeremiah 29:11-15).

Curses

Curses are essentially the opposite of the blessings listed above. Scriptural references to these cursings include:

"O LORD, God of our fathers, are you not the God who is in heaven? You rule over all the kingdoms of the nations. Power and might are in you hand, and no one can withstand you. (II Chronicles 20:6-7)

"The LORD is slow to anger, abounding in love and forgiving sin and rebellion. Yet he does not leave the guilty unpunished; he punishes the children for the sin of the fathers to the third and fourth generation. In accordance with your great love, forgive the sin of these people, just as you have pardoned them from the time they left Egypt until now.' The LORD replied, 'I have forgiven them, as you asked,'" (Numbers 14:18-20).

"Know that the LORD has set apart the godly for himself; the LORD will hear when I call to him," (Psalms 4:3).

"Come to me, all you who are weary and burdened, and I will give you rest. Take my yoke upon you and learn from me, for I am gentle and humble in heart, and you will find rest for your souls. For my yoke is easy and my burden is light," (Matthew 11:28-30).

"This is the confidence we have in approaching God: that if we ask anything according to his will, he hears us. And if we know that he hears us – whatever we ask – we know that we have what we asked of him," (1 John 5:14-15).

Curses, by definition mean to call down, to be made light of, small and contemptible, to pierce and cut (with ones words or actions). There are several Hebrew words which speak of this, but generally come from a similar root meaning.

Curses are transferred through lack of affirmation (neglect), or inappropriate affirmation such as abuse; physical, emotional, or sexual. When a child receives words of criticism, condemnation, put downs, etc., those messages can make an indelible negative impression on their tender psyche. If the child has a diminished sense of worth, and a limited sense of their importance for the future, discouragement, depression and despair can result. This is most evident in inner city and amongst certain ethnic people's communities who have been relegated by society; relegated to second class citizen status.

The negative affirmation or curse can open the door for psychological difficulty, and can place the individual in a vulnerable state of mind where demonic influences can occur. The importance of using great care in choosing our words and actions is so vital. May God help us all!

Talk of devils being confined to hell, or hidden by invisibility! -- We have them by shoals in the crowded towns and cities of the world. -- Talk of raising the devil! -- What need for that, when he is constantly walking to and fro in our streets, seeking whom he may devour.

- Anonymous -

Stan E. DeKoven, Ph.D.

Chapter Five

The Demonic Factor

I am not a demon chaser. I don't need to chase them... they show up on their own in very interesting ways, situations and times.

I am not one who believes that we should be constantly searching for demonic influences in people's lives. God has given to us the gift of discerning of spirits. With this gift we can determine the source of an individual's problem, whether demonic, the results of sin, or from physical or emotional malady.

As I have said I'm not a demon chaser, but I do recognize that there are spiritual forces of wickedness that must be dealt with in a Christian's life (as well as an unbeliever).

> *"Humble yourselves, therefore, under God's mighty hand, that he may lift you up in due time. Cast all your anxiety on him because he cares for you. Be self-controlled and alert. Your enemy the devil prowls around like a roaring lion looking for someone to devour. Resist him, standing firm in the faith, because you know that your brothers throughout the world are undergoing the same kind of sufferings,"* (I Peter 5:6-9).

Peter could have been speaking to those who suffer from the symptoms of dysfunctional family living. His statement could begin by saying, "Don't attempt to cover up the difficulties in your life, but instead humble yourselves under God's hand, and He will exalt you in the proper time."

I have become acutely aware of the need to allow God to take care of us. We need to cast all of our fear on Him because He does care for us. The admonition and the warning of Peter is very clear...we must become sober, or return to our right minds. That's easy to say but difficult to do.

Peter is not talking about sobriety in terms of alcohol usage or abuse. He is talking about being able to think clearly, being aware, being sure, steadfast in our thought process. Unfortunately, most people raised in dysfunctional families find this a most difficult task. We do not know what our right mind is.

Therefore, sobriety is something we desperately need and reach for in our relationships (co-dependent) through control, or through behavioral excess (such as overeating, drinking, working, sexing, etc.).

Looking again at the scripture we see that Peter states that we must first be humble, casting our cares upon Jesus.

Next, we must be willing to become sober or begin to think clearly (more on this later).

Of course, in the midst of our valiant attempts at clear thinking, the devil is trying to overcome us. We must learn how to resist him, to be firm or solid in our faith.

All believers experience times of suffering. God, through Christ, will deliver us. When a person chooses to deal with their problems in counseling or therapy, or seeks healing to their inner man, they will frequently experience suffering. What comes from the suffering will be great blessings for themselves, as well as for others that they relate to. It is worth the process.

Time, Place and Person

It has always been the purpose and plan of God to bring to His children into complete wholeness. To be complete in the Lord we must come to grips with the reality that iniquity, as we have defined it, continues to work its purpose, which is contrary to the purpose of God. Thus, we must develop a biblical strategy to destroy the chain of iniquity that binds up so many believers who have suffered from past trauma.

To see more clearly the spiritual dynamics involved in breaking the stronghold iniquity and subsequent patterns of destruction, let's look in at Satan's strategy.

> *"Then they brought him a demon-possessed man who was blind and mute, and Jesus healed him, so that he could both talk and see. All the people were astonished and said, 'Could this be the Son of David?' But when the Pharisees heard this, they said, 'It is only by Beelzebub, the prince of demons, that this fellow drives out demons.' Jesus knew their thoughts and said to them, 'Every kingdom divided against itself will be ruined, and every city or household divided against itself will not stand. If Satan drives out Satan, he is divided against himself. How then can his kingdom stand? And if I drive out demons by Beelzebub, by whom do your people drive them out? So then, they will be your judges. But if I drive out demons by the Spirit of God, then the kingdom of God has come upon you. Or again, how can anyone enter a strong man's house and carry off his possessions unless he first ties up the strong man? Then he can rob his house, '"* (Matthew 12:22-29).[6]

Jesus is speaking to the Pharisees after having delivered a man who was demon possessed, blind and dumb. His symptoms were linked by Christ to demonic activity. This was tremendous miracle, yet

---

[6] Of course, Jesus was primarily addressing the Pharisee's and their religious system but this teaching can apply to an individual as well.

Jesus was scoffed at and accused of casting out demons by the power of Satan.

In the 29th verse, Jesus gives us a clue as to how to deal with demonic forces. He says, *"Or again, how can anyone enter a strong man's house and carry off his possessions unless he first ties up the strong man? Then he can rob his house."*

Many of us have heard teaching on binding the strong man.

> *"I tell you the truth, whatever you bind on earth will be bound in heaven, and whatever you loose on earth will be loosed in heaven,"* (Matthew 18:18).

Jesus was instructing His disciples to take authority, bind or do not permit demonic forces the liberty to act or even speak. The authority to do so was given us in the name of Jesus Christ Himself.

This authority has been transferred to Christ's church, and thus we may now command evil forces in the name of Jesus, and they must do what we tell them to do! Ultimately, demonic forces must respond to the authority given to us by Christ since He is the Strongman who defeated evil by His resurrection.

Jesus is stating that to destroy, disrupt and overthrow demonic forces, we must first bind the strong man and then we can plunder (destroy) his house (or kingdom).

> *"When an evil spirit comes out of a man, it goes through arid places seeking rest and does not find it. Then it says, 'I will return to the house I left.' When it arrives, if finds the house unoccupied, swept clean and put in order. Then it goes and takes with it seven other spirits more wicked than itself, and they go in and live there. And the final condition of that man is worse than the first. That is how it will be with this wicked generation,"* (Matthew 12:43-45)

Jesus continues His teaching by focusing a little more directly on what happens in the spiritual realm. When we come to know Christ, demonic forces are expelled from our lives. However, the demonic forces that would have oppressed us try to control us and manipulate us still. Satan's plan is to keep us first from receiving Christ, and if that fails, to at least keep us from living our life in Him to its fullest.

The enemy attempts to attack us in various strategic ways. The Bible says this strong man has been bound and expelled by a stronger man. That stronger man, of course, is the Lord Jesus Christ by the power of the Holy Spirit.

When the demonic forces have been expelled, freedom is experienced and cleansing of our hearts occurs. Strategically, the unclean spirits follow a definite pattern. Verse 44 says *"I will return to my house."* In typical arrogant affirmation, **demonic forces believe that their house is your life**. The word "house" here means more than just an individual dwelling. It means "the generations of the family tree."

The Greek word used here is "oikia", meaning "family or household", and it is related to the Hebrew word "dowr" meaning "household or generation". When the new Christian is born again, all demonic activity must leave that believer's life. However, the demonic forces will come back to attempt to repossess the generation. This may occur in the believers' lifetime, or may wait until a more opportune time, in a future generation.

They attempt to repossess "their house" in the same areas of weakness that the individual believer's family tree has demonstrated weaknesses in prior generations.

Some Points to Remember

1. Recognize that the devil does not know everything, he is not everywhere at the same time. (not omniscient or omnipresent)

2. The enemy is NOT all powerful! (not omnipotent)! These characteristics belong to Almighty God alone!

3. The devil does have a very large and well trained army, with a specific desire to disrupt and destroy the things of God and the people of God.

One of the advantages demonic forces have over us is that they are not limited to time or place. Their life span continues generation after generation. They possess knowledge about us as individuals, and they know our family history, probably better than we do!

Have you ever wondered why it is that you are tempted in certain areas of life while other areas or temptations that seem to bother other believers never seem to cause you dismay? Do you think it is because somehow you are more blessed, stronger or better? This was one of the major concerns of our friend Joe. He suffered from various temptations and pervasive thoughts for which he could not find the origin. Why some temptations and not others?

Often the reason for this mystery is because you are not vulnerable in a certain area via your family tree. The multi-generational pattern or the family transmission system of psycho pathology, or from the spiritual viewpoint, the iniquity of the fathers are visited to the third and fourth generation. The visitors that come with it are the demonic forces. They have a strategic plan to attack, dismay, discourage, and disrupt the believer's life!

Satan's strategy is to thwart your growth, disrupt families, and destroy churches through attacking and influencing generational patterns. Idolatry and rebelliousness carry stiff penalties. They leave a family open to the influences of the demonic for countless years to come. Many families have these spirits "passed down" from generation to generation. The forces of darkness will gleefully ignore our legal standing as children of God for just as long as we allow them. The forces of darkness will capitalize on unconfessed sin. Rebellion and idolatry open the door for demonic harassment.

The cycle will continue until we confess our ancestor's sins of idolatry and rebelliousness so that they are wiped away by the blood of Jesus. There are certain things we must do to ensure that our generation and future generations will not be under the demonic attack in the areas of weakness. Whether we like to believe it or not, the reality is, the devil knows our weaknesses; he knows them because he's aware of our family patterns. The reason is simple.

Most of us come from families that are, or that were children of wrath by nature (Ephesians 2:3). They hated God by their behavior, even if they did so out of ignorance. Therefore, we are all under the course given us outlined in scripture.

It is so sad for me to talk to disappointed pastors and other family members who have been Christians their whole lives. Many have raised their families in the Christian doctrine, have loved their children well, and yet, when their children reach maturity, they go their own way. Often they live a life worse than any of their parents' experiences, to the great dismay of the family.

When you ask them questions about the previous generation or perhaps two generations before, you'll find similar behaviors occurring in the family tree. It becomes quite apparent that the iniquity of the prior generations has entangled them.

The devil knows these areas of weakness and vulnerability in our family tree. It is our responsibility as the Body of Christ to use our authority, as mandated by the Lord so that we no longer have to experience these curses, with the subsequent difficulties and the pain of our generational patterns.

Ultimately, we are all responsible for the choices we make and the directions we choose. It is difficult enough to live a life pleasing to God without this strategy of our enemy being active in out family trees. Thus, we must repent of ignorance and be willing to face and deal with this demonic strategy, and continue in the process of becoming all God has created us to be.

I have come back again to where I belong; not an enchanted place, but the walls are strong.

- Dorothy H. Rath -

Stan E. DeKoven, Ph.D.

Chapter Six

Recovery: The Way Back

The Discovery: The Search for Truth

One of the most painful things for all human beings to do is to look in the mirror. Even more painful than looking in the mirror is the process of looking into our own hearts and character. It is painful primarily for two reasons: One, because of the great shame and guilt we feel about the condition of our heart; and two, because of the lack of understanding concerning the character of God, His great power, mercy and grace.

In the book of I John, the great Apostle, called by scripture the beloved one, describes the character of God as having two primary characteristics: first is that of light; second, that of love.

> *"This is the message we have heard from him and declare to you: God is light; in him there is no darkness at all,"* (1 John 1:5).

> *"But if we walk in the light, as he is in the light, we have fellowship with one another, and the blood of Jesus, his Son, purifies us from all sin,"* (1 John 4:7).

The God of light exposes the darkness within our lives. All of us have areas of darkness, hidden agendas, misbeliefs, fears and negative attitudes that cause us great dismay and keep us from having a more intimate relationship with God the Father. I call these hidden fortresses.

When light begins to shine, it exposes those things which are in the darkness. Jesus wanted us all to become children of light, not children of darkness. As children of light, we must allow ourselves to be exposed to the light by the Word of God.

That process for many Christians is very difficult. We have been taught to believe that if one is caught doing something wrong, especially if one is caught in sin, rather than being cared for, nurtured, corrected and disciplined appropriately, we will be abuse, hurt, shamed and ridiculed.

This was certainly Mary's experience. As a 10 year old child, her haven of rest had always been school. Her home life would be classified as toxic, filled with verbal abuse, near abject poverty, and a woeful lack of intimacy and love. However, school, up until her 5th grade, had been a true place of safety.

In counseling she related an incident which sent her reeling, and from which she believed she would never recover. It was a normal day in her class, but his day would be different. Mary was a shy young girl, and against her will she was forced to stand up in front of the class and give an oral report. To this day she cannot remember the topic she was to present. Her fear was overwhelming, her shame unbearable, and in total panic she ran from the room. From that day she had hidden her feelings and protected her space with a vengeance. She learned so hide from everyone and everything, even from the light of God's word and the love of her Savior.

A large majority of the saints of God have learned to hide, to cover and defend against every possibility of coming to the light, even to the light of God. The fear of exposure is intense. There is no darkness in Him, and there is to be no darkness within the child of God.

Mary, like so many of us, expected the light to expose, and then she expected punishment and judgment of God to follow. The judgment we deserve was purchased by Christ on the cross! Jesus Christ took out shame and our guilt. Conditioned by past experience, we avoid the light rather than becoming transformed by God's love. For Mary, her fear of exposure and ridicule was extremely intense, but the symptoms which brought her to counseling were not just her own. She sought help fir herself and her whole family when she observed similar symptoms in her child and grandchild. To here surprise and dismay, these symptoms occurred in the absence of a precipitating even (the generational pattern).

Though we may expect punishment from our exposure to the light, God has another plan. Later in I John, the Apostle reveals the character of God as perfect, eternal, holy, wholesome with absolute unconditional love. Certainly God sees the sin, the discouragement, the unbelief, the heartache, the pain, the negative "stinkin' thinkin'" in our lives. Instead of punishing us, hurting us, condemning us, shaming us, He loves and forgives us and wills to heal us. Jesus has become the recipient of all the punishment that we deserve! However we must be willing to accept His full provision for us.

In this discovery section we are going to look at several models and principles for discovering the truth about our lives, and for receiving the love and nurturing of the Father we so desperately need.

The availability of the love of God for all believers has always been there. His light shows us the dark areas of our heart so we can present them to Him for transformation. Most people raised in dysfunctional families have difficulty receiving this truth because their ability to receive truth has been blurred by the dysfunction within the family. The models presented will assist in freeing us from past patterns of iniquity and prepare us to receive the totality of God's love.

"Search me O God and know my heart. Try me and know my thoughts (or my anxious thoughts) and see if there be any hurtful way in me and lead me in the everlasting way," (Psalm 139:23).

Psalm 51 contains David's famous prayer resulting from his sin with Bathsheba and murder of Uriah, her husband. It says,

"For the director of music. A psalm of David. When the prophet Nathan came to him after David had committed adultery with Bathsheba. Have mercy on me, O God, according to your unfailing love; according to your great compassion blot out my transgressions. Wash away all my iniquity and cleanse me from my sin. For I know my transgressions, and my sin is always before me. Against you, you only, have I sinned and done what is evil in your sight, so that you are proved right when you speak and justified when you judge. Surely I was sinful at birth, sinful from the time my mother conceived me. Surely you desire truth in the inner parts; you teach me wisdom in the inmost place. Cleanse me with hyssop, and I will be clean; wash me, and I will be whiter than snow. Let me hear joy and gladness; let the bones you have crushed rejoice. Hide your face from my sins and blot out all my iniquity. Create in me a pure heart, O God, and renew a steadfast sprit within me. Do not cast me from your presence or take your Holy Spirit from me. Restore to me the joy of your salvation and grant me a willing spirit, to sustain me. Then I will reach transgressors your ways, and sinners will turn back to you. Save me from bloodguilt, O God, the God who saves me, and my tongue will sing of your righteousness. O Lord, open my lips, and my mouth will declare your praise. You do not delight in sacrifice, or I would bring it; yhou do not take pleasure in burnt offerings. The sacrifices of God are broken spirit; a broken and contrite heart, O God, you

will not despise. In your good pleasure make Zion prosper; build up the walls of Jerusalem. Then there will be righteous sacrifices, whole burnt offerings to delight you; then bulls will be offered on your alter," (Psalms 51:1-19).

David, a man after God's own heart, recognized that within his heart were issues and agendas that were not pleasing to God. His prayer was that God would search his heart and his thoughts, especially his fearful thoughts, to see if there were any wicked ways, any iniquity within him. His prayer shows his desire to know and understand truth in the inner most part of his life (his self). His desire was to be fully cleansed and be made totally right with God.

David's prayer is a model for those wanting to overcome dysfunctional life patterns. We first must recognize that we need to have a scathing search of our heart. In the tradition of Alcoholics Anonymous' 12-step program, step 4 required fearless moral inventory. Sometimes this step can be most beneficial; at other times it can be diabolical, since we tend to become overwhelmed with the negative aspects of our character.

The Bible doesn't say for <u>you</u> to do a moral inventory, the Bible says the Holy Spirit does the moral inventory. Part of our recovery process is to discover the truth about ourselves. Not to do it via some invasive, psychological technique, but primarily through the loving process of allowing the Holy Spirit to graciously and gently reveal to us the truth by shining the light of God's Word in our hearts. If we are willing submit to the process, the issues of our heart that are to be dealt with by the power and love of God will be exposed for the process of transformation.

David's prayer should be our prayer: "Dear Lord God, search my heart, try my thoughts and show me if there is any wicked way. Lord give me truth in my inner man."

That is a difficult step to take, but it is one of the first ones that must be done if we are going to see God begin to work transformation for us.

We can see an example of the search for truth in the life of the Apostle Paul. Romans 7, is a scripture reference quoted by almost every believer who suffers from dysfunctional family patterns. Described is the conflict of the two natures.

> *"We know that the law is spiritual; but I am unspiritual, sold as a slave to sin. I do not understand what I do. For what I want to do I do not do, but what I hate I do,"* (Romans 7:14-15).

What a beautiful description, in a morbid sense, of the life of one raised in a dysfunctional family.

What a terrible life situation.

> *"And if I do what I do not want to do, I agree that the law is good,"* (Romans 7:16).

Our spirit has been made alive through Christ and is perfect, whole and complete. But, the spirit must come to the place where it controls the soul and the body.

The old nature is that part of a person which still remains subsequent to salvation. The soul (the mind, the will, and emotions), the conscience, as well as body, in which we still must work out our salvation with fear and trembling.

> *"I know that nothing good lives in me, that is, in my sinful nature. For I have the desire to do what is good, but I cannot carry it out,"* (Romans 7:18-24).

> *"For what I do is not the good I want to do; no, the evil I do not want to do – this I keep on doing. Now if I do what I do not want to do, it is no longer I who do it, but it*

is sin living in me that does it. So I find this law at work:
When I want to do good, evil is right there with me. For
in my inner being I delight in God's law; but I see
another law at work in the members of my body, waging
war against the law of my mind and making me a
prisoner of the law of sin at work within my members.
What a wretched man I am! Who will rescue me from this
body of death?" (Romans 7:19-23).

The Apostle Paul recognized there was a struggle that would continue in every believer's life, a struggle over which kingdom was going to have the preeminence. Would it be the carnal nature, the fleshly kingdom, the kingdom of self, or the kingdom of our Lord and of His Christ?

"Thanks be to God – through Jesus Christ our Lord! So
then, I myself in my mind an a slave to God's law, but in
the sinful nature a slave to the law of sin," (Romans
7:25).

It becomes necessary for us as individuals to deal with the old nature. It is the flesh, the old man, the old nature that is subject to the curses or consequences from our prior generations.

In the area of the soul, or our thought life, our will, our ability to make decisions and determine our directions, that the adversary will attack and oppress us. The devil knows that in our soul we are vulnerable to demonic influence and environmental impact. Therefore, we must be willing, as King David and the Apostle Paul, to search the inner man. Thus we allow the Holy Spirit to reveal the patterns that require transformation so we can walk though the process of change. Once we become aware, as illuminated by the Holy Spirit, we must then submit ourselves to the cross life and learn to render ourselves dead unto the old self and alive unto Christ (Romans 6:11).

A Final Look At Joe

Joe was willing to accept the need to look into his heart and allow the Holy Spirit to do His work of cleansing and deliverance. He had faith to believe that God was able, but not that God as his Father was willing. It took some time to convince Joe that the Father God who we served had little resemblance to his natural father. It took us several times of prayer together before he was able to receive the love of the Father, which finally came as the Lord revealed a very special memory to him.

When Joe was only 11, he had gone to Sunday school at a small church near his home. The church was Baptist, small and filled with men and women the average age of which was 70 years. Joe related that he enjoyed the Sunday school, the stories about Jesus, the times of singing, and especially the snack time at the end. There was one man that Joe remembered most. He was a deacon, he thought his name was Deacon Jones (doesn't every church have at least one). At first, the Deacon seemed to be a most stern character. He seemed to have his eye on Joe all the time. One day during one of the times Joe stayed for the adult service, Deacon Jones came and sat down next to Joe. He did not say anything to Joe, just sang with the congregation, read the Bible with the rest, and listened with an occasional amen to the sermon. Sometime after the singing and before the final amen, Joe would find himself laying his head against old Deacon Jones arm. Within no time, Deacon Jones, again without a word, would place his arm around Joe and hold him close. This ritual continued until it became no longer fashionable for Joe to "hang with the Deacon," but he never forgot the love and tenderness of this father figure.

In the counseling and healing prayer process, we were able to recreate the imagery of old Deacon Jones, and used this memory to relate to a Father who cared for Joe just the way he was. With this memory, long forgotten but always available to Joe and remembered by the Holy Spirit, we were able to let the light of the word of truth shine in Joe's heart which released the healing love of the Father God.

Stan E. DeKoven, Ph.D.

"Put on the full armor of God so that you can take your stand against the devil's schemes.

For our struggle is not against flesh and blood, but against the rulers, against the authorities, against the powers of this dark world and against the spiritual forces of evil in the heavenly realms.

Therefore put on the full armor of God, so that when the day of evil comes, you may be able to stand your ground, and after you have done everything, to stand."

- Apostle Paul -

Stan E. DeKoven, Ph.D.

Chapter Seven

Spiritual Warfare

The importance of spiritual warfare has been evident to the modern church. God has given you the power to bind and loose. Matthew 18:18 states,

> *"I tell you the truth, whatever you bind on earth will be bound in heaven, and whatever you loose on earth will be loosed in heaven."*

It is noteworthy the number of conferences being offered each year on this hot topic. There is more shouting, stomping, and contorting in the name of spiritual warfare, but the results are sometimes suspect. The fact is, we do warfare against spiritual wickedness in high places (Ephesians 6:12). However, our principle weapon of warfare is the establishment of God's Kingdom through effective personal evangelism and discipleship.

In our individual lives there comes times when the scheme or strategies of the hosts of hell must be encountered with the truth of God's Word. His Kingdom rule can take deeper root in our hearts. Thus, our spiritual warfare or strategy to counteract the strategy of Satan is addressed here. God's people are to take authority over the forces of darkness as an expression of our victorious life in Christ. Of special importance in our battle is the victory that comes through binding and loosing from emotional and spiritual bondages as they are revealed by the light of the Holy Spirit.

Quin Sherrer & Ruthanne Garlock, in *A Women's Guide to Spiritual Warfare*, page 139, use the term "Walking Free" to describe the process of loosing.

Walking Free:

"The bondages described in this chapter frequently entangle God's children and render them powerless in spiritual warfare. If the devil cannot get you to renounce your faith altogether, he will try to ensnare you with these traps and make you ineffective. Let us look at the steps we can take in order to walk free:

1. **Identify the problem area.** Ask the Holy Spirit to show you any areas of bondage you may have overlooked. You must be willing to acknowledge past ties that bind as the Holy Spirit reveals them.

2. **Confess and repent** before the Lord the sins the Holy Spirit reveals to you. This includes renouncing the past ties.

3. **Choose to forgive** all who have wounded you; also forgive yourself. Release your anger toward God, your feeling that he 'let you down.' In the process, claim afresh your total obedience to Jesus Christ as your Savior and Lord.

4. **Receive God's forgiveness and cleansing**, and pray specifically to walk in the opposite of the past cursing.

5. **Renounce the sin and close the door** in any area where the enemy has gained entry.

6. **Ask the Holy Spirit to help you break the behavior** and thought patterns you've become accustomed to (see Phil. 4:7-9).

7. **Allow the Holy Spirit to daily conform you** to the image of Christ."

A balance is required between the need to take authority over demonic forces and the need to overcome our flesh by the power of God's Word and our personal choices. Both the demonic influence and the deeds of the flesh must be presented to Christ and His cross.

The power of God through the cross is available and more than adequate to bring us into freedom in Christ. However, we must be willing to cooperate with the Holy Spirit in the process of our warfare. Dr. Neil Anderson writes in his booklet, *Steps to Freedom in Christ*, another approach to our process of change. He presents 7 steps that believers who have been victims (or anyone raised in a dysfunctional family) can pray through, with a concerned mature believer which will lead to victory.

The steps with commentary by the author include:

1. **Counterfeit versus Real** entails denouncing any previous or current involvement in occultic activity or false religions. Of course, you must know if you or members of your family tree have been involved (in the occult); so a good family tree inventory that relies on the Holy Spirit to reveal truth is necessary. If counterfeit beliefs exist, the prayer of agreement, bringing the false to the cross, followed by replacing the counterfeit with the truth found in God's Word will bring liberty.

2. **Deception versus Truth** is a process of allowing the Holy Spirit and God's Word to reveal falsehoods, or lies that we desire to be true. We will often allow our hearts (seat of emotions) to unwisely rule our minds, and our carnal mind then provides justification (defenses) for our self-centered heart[7]. The Lord wants us to embrace the truth; we must know the truth and choose to obey. Our first step in obedience is to submit ourselves to a process of change, seek the truth, and bring all deception to the cross of Christ.

3. **Bitterness versus Forgiveness** is when we choose to forgive those who have wronged us, understanding that "feeling" like forgiving or "feeling" like you have forgiven will follow

---

[7] For more on this see Sanford and Sanford, *Renewal of the Mind*. Victory House, 1991

119

your prayer of obedience. This will be discussed more thoroughly because of its importance under the section on "Family Forgiveness."

4. **Rebellion versus Submission**. We must recognize that any rebellion against legitimate authority is contrary to scripture. Submitting ourselves, first through prayer, confession of our failures, and then through obedience, to all legitimate authority, will provide liberty.

5. **Pride versus Humility**. Neal Diamond performed a song many years ago with a line that has stuck with me for years. He sings, "Pride is the chief cause in the decline in the number of husbands and wives." There is truth in that statement.

We know that pride is a destructive attitude and mindset that is at the root of most other sins. Pride goes before destruction (Proverb 16:18). The symptoms of pride are described with clarity by Floyd McClung in his book *Holiness and the Spirit of the Age*.

His primary points indicating the possibility of pride include:

- Impatience when inconvenienced, causing frustration, anger or even explosiveness.

- Avoiding of "troublesome" people.

- Difficulty in forgiving others (when demanding allowances for oneself)

- Being demanding and carrying an attitude of superiority.

- Using sarcastic humor at the expense of others

- Being judgmental and having a critical spirit

- Being hardhearted toward others

- Having envy, jealousy which can lead to greediness

- Being thoughtless of others. Being untouchable or a know-it-all

- Disloyal to others, especially your superiors

- A people pleasure (co-dependent, seeking to please so your needs can be met)

- A person with self-pity, feeling sorry for oneself, victimized

- Self-righteous and legalistic

As you can see, pride can be a major problem that can infect us all. Pride is what kept me from reaching out to my father after I knew I needed to out of obedience to God and His Word. Pride is a destroyer.

The cure for pride is humility, the willingness to submit oneself to the Lordship of Christ. It is bringing the self-life to the cross to allow our selfishness and arrogance to be swallowed up in Christ's love. Continuing on with Neil Andersons' prescription;

6. **Bondage versus Freedom** focuses on overcoming habitual sin. This includes breaking the bondage from the past and facing the deeds of the flesh with the truth of God's Word. More on this later.

7. **Acquiescence versus Renunciation** discusses your generational patterns. This will be the primary focus of our "The Prayer" section which is to follow.

There has been much teaching of late on spiritual warfare and the authority of the believer. A portion of this teaching includes the power of binding and loosing. A strategic area of this teaching is eradicating the power of our generational curses. At the end of this chapter, you will have opportunity to activate God's healing through two different prayers.

In the first prayer, we will ask the Holy Spirit to reveal to you the areas of your heart and mind that need transformation. These will be the areas where you have had difficulty, or dysfunction, and may be a part of a generational pattern of iniquity. These may be targets for the devil's attack. In this prayer, you will take authority over any pattern of iniquity defeat the devil. Further, you will permit the Spirit of God to move into the vacuum created, to fill you with light and love. This will allow you to be free from any past bondage.

Of course, there is no magic in this!

This will be a beginning for many of you. Over time, and often with the assistance of trained counselor, you will become aware of how the devil may still attack, and hopefully, you will commit to the process of preparing and strengthening yourself through the Word. Two questionnaires have been provided for you in the appendix of this book to help you "uncover" areas you will target for prayer. Again, it is recommended that you process through this with a mature prayer partner, to insure accountability and thoroughness.

Secondly, we are going to have a prayer of cleansing of the sins of the negative seed or the wrong behaviors and patterns that have been placed within your life. This will be done once and for all. All believers need to have a point in time when they can categorically state that we have faced sin, nailing them as it were to the cross. Jesus' blood cleanses us from all sin, past, present, and future.

Romans 8:1 says,

> *"There is therefore now no condemnation for those who are in Christ Jesus."*

That is a complete declaration. Regardless of where we have been and what we have done, we are free in Christ! The prayer we will pray will help us establish at this point in time our freedom and our liberty through the efficacy of Jesus Christ and His blood. Following the prayer, which is the beginning of our healing, more will be presented to assist in the continuing process of restoration.

Prayer Is Vital

Prayer is a vital and viable force in bringing healing to the soul. The scripture reference first mentioned in the author's foreword, Malachi 4:6, speaks of the promise of restoration. The Lord is restoring to the Church its power, glory, doctrinal purity, and the family.

It is exciting to observe all that is occurring in light of the times we live in. Most, if not all, Christians are anticipating the soon return of the Lord Jesus Christ. However, the return could be delayed due to the fractured nature of His spiritual body, the family of God.

In preparation for His return, the Gospel must be preached to all nations, and the hearts of the fathers and the children must be transformed by God's power, grace, mercy and love. That which we need to bind is the influence of the devil in problematic areas of our lives. However, we first must know what areas of our life and generational histories need addressing.

I urge you to begin now to ask the Holy Spirit to reveal to you the areas of your life that the devil may have access to because of generational sins (iniquity). If need be, ask your parents, ask your grandparents (if they are still alive) what events from the past may have opened a door of opportunity for temptation.

What events, what difficulties, what problems did they experience? Be willing to face these problems without denial. Do not take them lightly, but write them down and compare them with the passages of scripture in Deuteronomy that we have already reviewed.

Determine in an unscathingly manner what areas need cleansing and healing in your life. If you do not become honest with yourself, you will not grow in truth and freedom. It is a difficult process, and you may need a trusted partner to work with. Preferably an elder or counselor should be found who can assist you in your search for truth. They will help you see areas of need and help you pray them through.

Once you have done your note taking, and determined the areas of weakness, then you will need to pray. When you pray, you need to pray in faith in the power of God. It is not the amount of the shout that counts, but the level of faith in the power of God and His Word that matters. You may want to join with a prayer warrior who can help you to come against and to break the demonic cords of oppression that may have been placed upon your life.

Again, I will present to you a pattern prayer at the end of this section. When you pray, pray confessing both your known sin, and the sin of all generations. It is important to pray for forgiveness, and come against, bind, and break any cord, any curse, any negative influence of the past.

You will take authority over them in the name of Jesus, and accept His blood that cleanses from all sin!

Once you have completed this prayer, proclaim your liberty in Christ! Our goal is total release and then to experience our freedom in our walk with Christ.

According to Mark Johnson (Johnson, M. Spiritual Warfare for the Wounded. p. 68.), release from bondage comes the following procedure:

1. Define the content of the lies and the spirit responsible (lust, fear, etc.).

2. Separate from them by repenting. Bind the power of demonic forces in Jesus' Name.

3. Refute the lie with truth; exchange the lie for the truth. Johnson also suggested a four step process to healing (Johnson, pages 157-159). They are:

    • Regression - Recall past events as led by the Holy Spirit.

    • Revision - Revise your old thought patterns bringing them into line with God's Word.

- Resolution - Resolving the grief process[8].

- Reconciliation - Forgiveness and release.

The Prayers

Rather than one encompassing prayer, it seems appropriate to have several sessions of prayer. When doing so, it is highly recommended that you pray with a seasoned veteran who can agree with you and assist in the process.

There is no time limit. You should pray in a safe and secure place where there will be no interruptions. This is serious business that demonic forces will want to stop if possible.

Remember, all demonic forces are already under our feet, defeated forever by the death and resurrection of Christ!

We will pray in the following order: First, the prayer of Renunciation; next, Repentance; then, Restoration; finally Recommitment.

1. Renunciation

Rather than just read this prayer, recite it out loud! From this prayer, develop one of your own using this as a model. Use your own words that reveal the issues in your life. As you pray, believe God for a great release.

I believe with all my heart, in agreement with you, that God is going to do a great and mighty work in your life.

---

[8] See *Grief Relief* by Dr. Stan DeKoven.

Here is the pattern prayer:

Dear Heavenly Father,

I thank You in the name of Jesus Christ that You have given us salvation through Christ. I thank You Lord that because I confessed with my mouth the Lord Jesus Christ and believed in my heart that You raised Him from the dead that I am saved. I am well aware that salvation is both an event and also a process. I believe Lord you are bringing me to a place of wholeness and completeness through Christ.

Lord, I recognize that though the devil has been kicked out of my generation, those spirits that were attacking and were negatively influencing areas in my family in generations past, whether spiritually, genetically or environmentally, would like to come back and hurt me in this generation. They also have plans in the next generation.

Father, I thank You. I am aware, I have knowledge and now have wisdom. Thus I can acknowledge that Christ given authority over every demonic force in the name of Jesus Christ of Nazareth, by the power of the Holy Spirit. I confess that Jesus Christ is Lord and that He came in the flesh. I speak now in the name of Jesus and affirm my authority over every demonic force in the name of Jesus Christ.

I also acknowledge authority over any pattern of iniquity that would harm my family or me due to idolatry or dishonoring of parents or lack of hospitality, lust and immorality, the mistreating of neighbors, bribery or not keeping the law. Lord God, any areas that I have been in sin in those areas in the past I confess now in the name of Jesus, and I repent of the chain of iniquity, in Jesus' name!

In the name of Jesus, according to your Word, I declare that I am free from the curse of barrenness!

In the name of Jesus, I declare that I am free from guilt and the curse of guilt!

I declare that I am free of disease and infirmity, cancer, alcoholism, and drug abuse.

Any spirit of despair, disappointment, any curse from it, I break you in Jesus' name.

I declare that I am free of adversity; I break you in Jesus' name.

The lack of peace and comfort, I declare that I am free from you in the name of Jesus!

Bondage of any kind, I declare that I am free from you and I break you in the name of Jesus!

Poverty and sickness, in the name of Jesus, I declare that I am free from you and I break you in Jesus' name!

Hard heartedness and powerlessness, you curse that comes because of the sins of the father, in the name of Jesus, I declare that I am free from all of you. I command you now in Jesus' name, you no longer have access to my generation, my "house."

Now I take authority over any thought from having any influence upon my family, my generation, past, present and future. I take authority right now in the name of Jesus and I loose the love, the Spirit, the power, and the nurturing of God to bring healing and restoration into my heart. Strong man, you are bound in the name of Jesus, you have no authority over me. From this moment on I claim my generation and subsequent generations free! Amen!

The Cleansing

When I first began to pray this prayer after teaching on the generational iniquity and their influence, God began to do some tremendous things. In my life and in thousands of precious people in various nations of the world, freedom in Christ as never before began to occur. We live in a time where we cannot afford, either financially or with our resources of time, to take weeks, months and even years to bring about restoration of people's hearts.

We need to allow the power of God to flow and to break these curses, to establish liberty in those that were held captive. But we need to go even deeper.

The results of sin can continue to carry negative effects in our lives. Therefore, it is essential to look in the mirror, and review the difficulties caused by choices we have made based upon faulty life patterns.

For complete liberty, we must begin to face ourselves the way God would want us to.

For many Christians, as we face our fleshly nature, we have two choices: 1) we can project blame and become bitter, or 2) we can receive the truth and take responsibility for our lives. For most of us who have been raised in a dysfunctional family, notwithstanding the cause, we have had reinforced many times over the necessity to blame and develop bitterness as a way to cope with our pain.

God wants to replace the roots of bitterness and anchor us in His love.

> *"See to it that no one misses the grace of God and that no bitter root grows up to cause trouble and defile many,"* (Hebrews 12:15).

A heart that has developed bitterness becomes hardened and unable to be responsive to the Word or Spirit of God as the Lord would intend. Therefore, we need to do more than just break the curses and take authority over the devil, which hopefully all of you have done. We need to be willing to look at our present life, our continuing areas of sin, and be willing to note them. Once noted, we can take the next step in our restoration process, which continues through healing prayer and the application of the Word of God.

Wholeness is God's Idea

"My dear brothers, take note of this: Everyone should be quick to listen, slow to speak and slow to speak and slow to become angry, for man's anger does not bring about the righteous life that God desires," (James 1:19-20).

The anger of man includes projection of blame and bitterness, and can also include acting out or rejecting the truth. Verse 21 says,

"Therefore, get rid of all moral filth and the evil that is so prevalent and humbly accept the word planted in you, which can save you."

The word salvation here is the same word for initial salvation, the word *sozo*. It means "to become whole, to become complete." Becoming whole begins at initial salvation, and continues as a life long process. When we receive the Word of God with humility, recognizing that it is but for the grace of God that we even live, and we take God at His Word, applying it to our lives, the transformation of our inner man begins.

"Do not merely listen to the word, and so deceive yourselves. Do what it says," (James 1:22).

The defensive stance of one who is deluded is the projection of blame. A deluded person will not face truth, but projects responsibility to avoid pain. Instead of looking at themselves, they always blame others for their problems. It is so easy and natural for us as human beings to place responsibility on others, when in many cases the responsibility belongs to us. There can be situations where the responsibility belongs to others (such as child abuse). Yet even then, as adults, we must take responsibility for that which belongs to us, which is our response in the present to our painful past.

That is why we need to search for truth. We need to be doers of the Word and not hearers only. We need to take what the Word of God says and apply it to our lives, acting on it:

> *"Anyone who listens to the word but does not do what it says is like a man who looks at his face in a mirror and, after looking at himself, goes away and immediately forgets what he looks like, But the man who looks intently into the perfect law that gives freedom, and continues to do this, not forgetting what he has heard, but doing it – he will be blessed in what he does, "* (James 1:23-25).

What we need as individuals raised in dysfunctional families are the blessings of God. The blessings of God come, according to God's Word, when we become an effectual doer of that which we have heard. As we live according to the law of liberty, as we are willing to look at ourselves in the mirror and present ourselves humbly before the Lord, God will transform us.

It is important to understand that the process of change is really the process of repentance. The word "repent" means "a change of thinking that leads to a change of lifestyle."

James 5, outlines a process for people to receive the healing and restoration that they need.

> *"Is anyone among you suffering? Let him pray. Is anyone cheerful? Let him sing praises. Is anyone among you sick? Let him call for the elders of the church, and*

let them pray over him, anointing him with oil in the name of the Lord. And the prayer offered in faith will restore the one who is sick, and the Lord will raise him up, and if he has committed sins, they will be forgiven him. Therefore, confess your sins to one another, and pray for one another, so that you may be healed. The effective prayer of a righteous man can accomplish much," (James 5:13-16).

This passage greatly relates to our cleansing process. In the 13th verse it says, *"Is any among you suffering? Let him pray."* Often when Christians are going through pain, especially the painful remorse of a damaged past, rather then praying, calling upon God, they run around and talk to anybody and everybody who will listen. Seeking constant counsel can be a method of avoidance, to keep from facing ourselves honestly. We need to encourage prayer in the Body of Christ for those who suffer.

"Is anyone cheerful? Let him sing praises." Preferably to himself. *"Is anyone among you sick?"* The word "sickness" here includes sickness of the soul, sickness of the spirit or sickness in the body. In all of those cases, we are to call for the elders, the mature ones of the church, and let them pray over us, anointing with oil. Oil was used both as a symbol of the Holy Spirit and of the anointing of God, but it was also used as a medicinal ointment. It is perfectly acceptable to use the best of medicine, behavioral science and prayer, believing God for great things.

The Word says the prayer offered in faith will restore the one who is sick. Obviously, we must have faith -- a belief, understanding or knowing that what we are asking of God He will do because it is according to His will.

Remember Mary

When it came time for us to really pray with Mary, she was filled with initial fear. She had never been very good at opening up and sharing her feelings. However, she could clearly see the chain of iniquity in her life, and she wanted to walk in a new freedom (as well as to take this freedom to her family),

Very quietly and sweetly we began to pray a prayer of faith on her behalf. The confession of faults or sins had been an ongoing process, but this day she was ready to let go of her need to keep her pain and release it to the Lord. Our prayer for her was simple, that Jesus would enter into the place of pain in her life and free her from all that bound her. She also prayed, confessing her sin, the generational patterns, and asking for forgiveness for holding on to her bitterness against her teacher, the other students (who laughed at her calamity) and at the Lord for allowing it to happen. Many other items needing cleansing, such as her relationship with her mother and father, etc. also surfaced during the time of prayer. This is often the case, and we brought these to the foot of the cross as well.

Though the freedom was not instantaneous, it was distinctive. From the moment she allowed the Father to love her, things began to change. It was the beginning of many other times of cleansing and deliverance that has made an incredible impact upon Mary and her whole family.

Most people raised in dysfunctional families suffer from discouragement. That is why it says in Colossians 3:21, "Fathers, provoke not your children *to anger*, lest they be discouraged." So much of the generational curse is the discouragement transmitted from the fathers. God wants to restore us back to our fathers. For this to be accomplished, there must come cleansing.

We must be willing to confess our sins and shortcomings, and do so in faith, believing God can meet our need.

How much faith do we need? Not much - just mustard seed faith. It is enough to say, "I believe that God can." The prayer of faith will restore the one who is sick. The word "restore" here means to be brought back to new, better than what they ever were. The Lord will heal the sick, and if there's sin, it will be forgiven. In other words, if sin (generational or personal) is the causative factor in our illness, that sin will be forgiven and our lives will be healed.

Forgiveness and cleansing come as we are forgiven.

The Bible also says we must forgive others. Forgiveness will be discussed in greater detail in the next chapter of this book. *"Therefore confess your sins to each other,"* (James 5:16a). The "each other" presented here really has to be understood within the context of the elders. We are not to just confess to anybody who will listen, because many people who listen are looking for good gossip to pass onto others. Many Christians have been hurt because of sins unwisely confessed to people who could not be trusted. Further, the confession should never be forced before we are ready, this would be another violation of our boundaries, and create new wounds and betrayal. Confess only to the mature who meet the qualifications found in I Timothy and Titus as elders and deacons within a local church. Confess to one another and pray for one another so that you may be healed.

"The effective prayer of a righteous man can accomplish much," (James 5:16b, NASB). Effective prayer means prayer that hits the mark. We can only pray to the mark if we know what the mark is. Therefore, we need the Holy Spirit to reveal the issues of the heart. Once the Holy Spirit reveals something, we need a prayer of faith that hits the mark, that is fervent, so it will accomplish what needs to be accomplished for the glory of God.

2. Repentance

In this prayer, your goal is to begin to change the beliefs about the past, and confront an unbiblical, carnal heart. You will take authority over your heart and command it to submit to the Holy Spirit.

Again, "repentance" means "a change of thinking that leads to a change in life style." Before praying, you will want to review again with a caring believer the wrong beliefs, improper attitudes, sinful patterns. Then in humility cast down (II Corinthians 10:4-6) those worthless thought patterns, bringing them into obedience.

This vital step in your healing process will continue daily as you walk in liberty with Christ and your fellow believers.

Prayer of Repentance

Let me encourage you to take time to pray a prayer of repentance, using the following as a model.

Dear Father,

According to Your Word I submit myself to You. I admit that my thought life, my old carnal nature has ruled my heart, and I submit my heart to You.

In Jesus' Name, I cast down the worthless beliefs of wickedness of (name them specifically) and ask You to forgive me and cleanse me. I freely choose to obey Your Word and daily bring my sinful thoughts and feelings to the cross that I might freely, without condemnation daily in Your presence.

I thank You for Your cleansing and strength.

Holy Spirit, renew my mind by washing it with Your Word. I praise You, Father, for my cleansing, in Jesus' name, Amen!

As stated before, this prayer should become a comfortable one for you. As we walk with the Lord and mature in Christ, you will find other areas of sin that need to be dealt with. As you do so, out of obedience to God's Word, He will continue to cleanse you and give you the mind of Christ.

The family was ordained of God that children might be trained up for Himself; it was before the church, or rather the first form of the church on earth.

- Pope Leo XIII -

Stan E. DeKoven, Ph.D.

Chapter Eight

Family Forgiveness

Forgiveness - 70 times 7

Not only must we confess faults and sins in our prayer of repentance, we must be willing to forgive and receive forgiveness. In dealing with the issue of forgiveness, I think it is important to look primarily at the teaching of Jesus Himself. In Matthew 6:14-15 which follows the pattern prayer called "the Lord's Prayer," it reads:

> *"For if you forgive men when they sin against you, your heavenly Father will also forgive you. But if you so not forgive men their sins, your Father will not forgive your sins."*

All of us have been taught that forgiveness is a vital and important aspect of our life in God. I believe with all of my heart we need to forgive those who have hurt us, and we must seek reconciliation and forgiveness from others when we have hurt them.

However, there are certain limitations to our ability to forgive with the purpose of facilitating restoration of reconciliation of relationship. For instance, in the book of Luke, the 17th chapter, Jesus is speaking to His disciples. Jesus states that it is inevitable that stumbling blocks should come, but woe to him through whom they come. It would be better for him if a millstone were hung around his neck and he were thrown into the sea than that he should cause one of these little ones to stumble.

Be on your guard! If your brother sins, rebuke him; **if he repents**, forgive him.

This passage parallels Matthew, chapter 18. It continues,

> *"If he sins against you seven times in a day, and seven times comes back to you and says, 'I repent,' forgive him,"* (Luke 17:4).

This was a very difficult challenge Jesus gave. The standard of the day was if someone sins against you, and then asks for forgiveness, you forgive him up to 7 times. On the 8th time, that is it! You treat him as an unbeliever or a heathen.

Jesus expanded the law of liberty and the law of love, saying forgiveness should be part of our lifestyle.

The difficulty in being able to forgive those who have hurt us is two-fold. First, there can be an unwillingness, or a fear to confront someone who has hurt us. Second, there is an unwillingness of the individuals who have hurt us to repent so that forgiveness can occur.

The Bible indicates in Matthew 18 and in Luke 17 that our responsibility is to forgive, but forgiveness comes when we go through the process of confronting the wrong. However, if some one who has wronged you is unwilling to admit and repent, forgiveness that leads to reconciliation is not possible (otherwise, how can you trust if there is no repentance?)

You can forgive them before the Lord, and release them to Him. For those who have been severely abused or molested, it is important to recognize that the responsibility for the molestation is on the abuser, especially if the abuse was against a young child. The young child had no responsibility in the abuse process; the adult abuser is always responsible. Because of the dynamics of that relationship, confrontation is not always possible or wise. In cases like this, we can only forgive from our heart before the Lord (preferably with a special prayer partner) and leave the pain there. Trust, or relationship, may not, and in most cases, should not be reestablished with the offending person.

Where confrontation is possible and advised, it should be done from a position of strength, reality, and humility. Our strength is in the truth of God and His Word, reality is knowing that there is no guarantee of living "happily ever after," and humility is understanding that no one deserves forgiveness, including ourselves.

Forgiving Mom and Dad

It is a frightening thing to talk to parents. I remember the first time I confronted my mom and dad about things that had happened in my family. When I say "confrontation," I just mean "to expose, to bring to the surface, to make plain." When I made things plain and clear to them from my perspective, I learned many new things.

For one, I learned that my memory was far from perfect. I had to admit I probably was not as righteous as I thought. Many things that I believed had happened just the way I perceived them I later found were misquoted or misunderstood. Even though I did not always remember with perfect accuracy, my perception of hurt and pain were just as real and valid, and I still needed to talk them through to a place of understanding and forgiveness.

Thus, I was able to bring things to the surface and give my parents an opportunity to respond, reflect, and explain and in some instances repent and ask for forgiveness. At that point, forgiveness was very easy because it was already in my heart to do.

Getting to Know You

Before I could forgive and release my father for not being perfect, I first had to get to know him. His character, motivations, history and life experiences that helped shape the man I know as father remained a mystery to me. To my dad's credit, he was willing to share much of who he was and is with my sister, brother and me, which has given us all insight and understanding. Our appreciation of him and my mother has grown. We have embraced fully their life stories and how their experiences led to the family dynamics we were raised with.

For forgiveness and cleansing of the heart to occur, a knowledge of the father is essential. This may happen in a number of ways; the best is a personal encounter called a confrontation. This encounter does not need to be difficult or painful, but needs to be thorough enough to lead to understanding. (Included in Appendix 1 is a sample questionnaire you might use as a model for your confrontation.)

I recognized that, given the circumstances of their lives, my parents did the best they knew how to do. In many ways, they were marvelous parents, especially when you consider the deficits they brought into their marriage. So, I had no right to punish them, though they were responsible for some difficulties in my life. My confrontation of those things brought the opportunity to bring forgiveness and ultimately healing as I released them of responsibility for the things they had done. At the same time, there were other people who, regardless of confrontation, would never admit; never repent. What do we do with them?

From my understanding of the scriptures, the best we can do is to forgive them before the Lord and release them to God. But in terms of reconciliation in relationship, it probably is not possible until such time as they are willing to face, admit and repent from their wrongdoing.

Be careful here. We do not sit in a place of judgment or superiority, but we humbly submit ourselves unto the Lord, confessing before Him that we have done our part. It is now up to them to do whatever it is they are going to do. We must be mature enough to forgive others of the offences they have caused us.

The greatest difficulty comes in being able to forgive ourselves!

The Bible never says we are to forgive ourselves. In fact, we can only receive the forgiveness of God. To receive the forgiveness of God means we must be humble before the Lord. It is not a prideful statement to say "I have been forgiven by God, I'm free."

That is a statement of humility. The greatest form of pride is to believe we are so important that we can hold a grudge against God, or to hold ourselves up as sinners higher than God's grace ("God cannot forgive me. My sin is too big!").

We no longer have to try and prove any longer how bad we are. God knows our heart. He has forgiven ALL my sins. That's enough.

Walking in Forgiveness

If the rest of the world does not accept us, it really doesn't matter. We must receive forgiveness ourselves, because God has forgiven us. This final step is one Paul knew well. Before he became Paul he was Saul, the murderer. I cannot imagine the level of condemnation, guilt, remorse, shame, and fear Paul must have carried because of his former behavior. Yet, he was a man with a powerful ministry who was able to shake the nations for Christ. Paul stated;

> Romans 8:1, it says, *"Therefore, there is now no condemnation for those who are in Christ Jesus."*

> In Romans 12:1-2, it says, *"Therefore, I urge you, brothers, in view of God's mercy, to offer your bodies as living sacrifices, holy and pleasing to God – this is your spiritual act of worship. Do not conform and longer to the pattern of this world, but be transformed by the renewing of your mind. Then you will be able to test and approve what God's will is – his good, pleasing and perfect will."*

The Apostle Paul, as most preachers, did not preach or teach what he had not experienced. He preached and taught by the revelation of God out of his experiences. We can assume Paul probably went through a time where he had to have his mind renewed -time of transformation and change. He presented himself as a living sacrifice before the Lord. He humbled himself before God. He allowed his mind to be renewed by the washing of the water with the Word.

As Paul later wrote, he put off the old, renewed his mind, and put on the new (Ephesians 4:24). He began a walk in the grace and mercy of God. In doing so, he was able to prove that God was working out His perfect will in his life. In II Corinthians 10 the Apostle Paul speaks, describing himself again. He says;

> *"By the meekness and gentleness of Christ, I appeal to you – I, Paul, who am 'timid' when face to face with you, but 'bold' when away! I beg you that when I come I may not have to be as bold as I expect to be toward some people who think that we live by the standards of this world. For though we live in the world, we do not wage war as the world does,"* (II Corinthians 10:1-3).

The Apostle Paul had many who spoke against him! Much of this letter is written to the church not only to correct over-zealous church discipline, but to represent himself as an Apostle to the Gentiles. He speaks with meekness and gentility, yet carries an anointing of God. He recognized that, just like his audience, he was subject to the normal problems of natural life.

Paul had apparently traversed through the process discussed in Ephesians 4. He had renewed his mind.

> *"For though we live in the world, we do not wage war as the world does. The weapons we fight with are not the weapons of the world. On the contrary, they have divine power to demolish strongholds,"* (II Corinthians 10:3-4).

Further, Paul presents a powerful truth to the church. The Bible states that we *have* the armor of God (Ephesians 6). We have spiritual weapons available to us, including the shield of faith, the helmet of salvation, the breastplate of righteousness, the belt of truth, and feet shod with the preparation of the gospel of peace. We also have the sword of the spirit, which is the Word of God.

Paul states, "We don't war against the flesh by fleshly principles, but through the Spirit by faith, by the Word of God."

This is the process we began in our prayers on deliverance and release in the last chapter.

Paul encourages believers to continue the battle in our mind by tearing down fortresses, destroying the strongholds of the devil. This must be done to insure our continued growth in the Lord, and to continue in our process of maturation.

> *"We demolish arguments and every pretension that sets itself up against the knowledge of God, and we take captive every thought to make it obedient to Christ. And we will be ready to punish every act of disobedience, once your obedience is complete,"* (II Corinthians 10-5-6).

There are many things that compete for our thoughts. They include speculations, desires, philosophies, anything from the past or present, anything we have learned or experienced that says something contrary to or lifts itself above the truth found in God's Word.

The Bible says any thought above God is a lie and is akin to idolatry.

Paul, recognizing the diabolic nature of these things, says that we are to destroy speculations. In another place, he tells us to practice "casting them down." That means "to speak them, to confess them", not to confess to possess, but to speak them out of ourselves by taking authority over them in the name of Jesus.

We are to punish all disobedience and take every thought captive. Any thought about the self, the world, about other Christians or about God Himself that does not line up with the truth of the Word of God is to be brought into Godly submission. As it were, we must take them captive and imprison them.

How? By speaking it, by saying it is so, in the name of Jesus. For example, you might declare, "You negative thought, I reject you from my mind in the name of the Lord Jesus!" Perhaps a small example will bring this principle greater clarity.

You may be walking down the street and happen to look inside a car window. Sitting on the seat is a $20.00 bill. The door is unlocked, the window is down, and the thought comes to your mind, "Gee this could be a blessing from God! Thank you, Lord, I needed twenty dollars!"

Well, that obviously is not a thought pleasing to God because God never allows stealing. The Bible declares, *"Thou shalt not steal!"*

So, what do you do with that thought? Most of us raised in dysfunctional families will banter back and forth, wondering "Was it God or was it not God? Should I, shouldn't I, should I, shouldn't I?" Rather than facing the truth of God's Word, we debate with our mind and the devil.

If you do anything, you should try and find the owner of the car so they can protect their valuables. Certainly, you should never entertain the thought of stealing. Take that thought captive!

You might say, "You thought of stealing, wherever you came from, I bind you in Jesus' name. I'm not going to think that way. I'm a child of God and I do not steal." That is taking thoughts captive and bringing them to the obedience of Christ!

Recognize evil thoughts as an enemy. Condemn these negative thoughts, that stinking thinking from the past, that ego-centric attitude that says "I need, I want, I wish, I, I, I, I." Take those thoughts captive and bring them under the obedience of Christ!

If we are going to say anything, we state, "I can do all things through Christ who strengthens me." You may state that, "I am the righteousness of God in Christ," or "I am a new creation in the Lord." As we take our thoughts captive, dealing with worthless thought patterns, and bring them unto the obedience of Christ, we do so with strength. The strength of the Holy Spirit, not our own strength, is required. Remember, *"for man's anger does not bring about the righteous life that God desires,"* (James 1:20).

The more we take authority over our thoughts, the stronger we become. We remain clean and walk in forgiveness, because we are going through this process every time we find a disobedient, errant thought. We begin to operate as members of the Kingdom by taking authority, confessing the truth, casting down imaginations, and punishing disobedient thoughts.

Then we enter into a position then where we can judge others according to their fruit. Yes, the Bible says in Matthew 7, *"Judge not lest you be judged."* So often we take that scripture out of context. What the Bible is talking about more than anything else is hypocrisy. We should not judge the fruit of someone else until we have dealt with similar issues in our own life.

Even when we do judge rightly, we should not judge harshly. We must not judge in terms of criticism, but judge with a purpose of evaluation so we are able to help a brother or sister who needs our perspective.

If we do see someone in sin, we need to speak to them in love. If we were pointing out an area of sin in someone else's life, and we had the same or a larger problem area in our own life, we would be hypocrites. We need to examine our own heart first, then we will have the clear insight to respond to the issues of our life, and in the lives of others.

The Bible says we are to judge according to the fruit.

> *"By their fruit you will recognize them. Do people pick grapes from thornbushes, or figs from thistles?"* (Matthew 7:16).

> *"Thus, by their fruit you will recognize them,"* (Matthew 7:20).

Negative seeds have been sown in your life, yet you need not despair. In the fullness of time God is working out all of those things in you so that you will bear fruit and your fruit will remain.

> *"As you abide in the vine, then His life will flow through you,"* (my paraphrase, see John 15).

The Prayer of Restoration

Now, let us pray a prayer of restoration.

> *Dear Father,*

> *I acknowledge my total dependence upon You. Without You, I can do nothing. I desire to be restored, reconciled to You and my family. Again, I take authority over my own worthless imaginations, and through the confession of my mouth, cast them down. I will no longer hold on to any bitterness, but choose to forgive my family, friends or enemies who have purposely or unwittingly hurt me (name specifically).*

> *I accept your restoring, healing love and light which is now being shed abroad in my heart. I bless those (do so specifically) who have cursed me and used me, and I*

release them from my critical judgment.

Thank You for Your freedom Lord, in Jesus' Name. Amen!

For I will restore health unto thee, and I will heal thee of thy wounds, saith the Lord.

- Old Testament: Jeremiah 30:17 -

Stan E. DeKoven, Ph.D.

Chapter Nine

The Healing

I hope by now it has been demonstrated that all believers need a process of sensing, of being set right, of becoming whole. For many, the healing process is both painful and time consuming. Very little healing occurs <u>only</u> with the passage of time. It is true that in certain psychological problems, such as certain depressions, given enough time, most people will just "get over it." However, the process takes at least twice as long that way as it will with help. It is far better to seek intervention and counseling to help the situation. Nonetheless, we must accept the fact that our healing process does take time.

It has taken many years to see the dysfunctional patterns fully developed in our lives. It will take time for healing.

For healing to take place, we must make some new choices. We must <u>choose</u> the search for truth, to define what is the meaning and essence of life. What misbeliefs have we held onto and confessed to be true when in reality they were lies from the devil or our old tapes(?? – pg 129 hardcopy)? We must take time to confront our wrong perceptions, and in many cases, confront those who have hurt us in the past. We must <u>choose</u> to forgive and release others of responsibility, for hurting us and ask for forgiveness from those we have harmed.

The Bible indicates that part of our healing comes as we let go of the things of the past by a grieving process. That process includes the recognition of what has happened, and the expression of the feelings that surround the event. It includes the eventual acceptance of our present life circumstances, embracing it as God's plan for our lives.

The Word also requires that we begin to walk by faith, not by sight. Christians still struggle. Even if they have gone through their time of healing prayer, taken their "40 days to the promise journey," have "put off the old man and renewed their mind," they will continue to struggle to move ahead in God.

It is very difficult to walk by faith and put one's complete trust in a God Who is there. Proverbs 3:5 and 6 says,

> *"Trust in the LORD with all your heart and lean not on your own understanding; in all your ways acknowledge him, and he will direct your paths straight."*

This is such a vital truth for those raised in dysfunctional families! The healing process occurs as we put our faith and trust in the goodness of God, His love and His divine plan for us.

I remember Jill, a wonderful Christian woman who had been abandoned by both her mother and father at a very early age. She took to therapy and healing prayer like a fish to water, and rapidly worked through her painful past with marvelous results. The final hurdle for her, and the release which lead to her greater wholeness, came as she finally realized that perfection was not her ultimate goal, but acceptance of the reality of God's love and acceptance of her just as she was. The fact that her righteousness was not what God required, but that Christ; righteousness was what she had to rest in, lead her to peace and joy, characteristics of the wonderful Kingdom of God. (Romans 14:17).

Our God is a God of design, plan, purpose and objectives. God does have a plan for us! Most of our lives, before we knew Christ, and even for a significant time after, was chaotic. There were no clear boundaries, nothing we could really put our faith and trust in.

But we know God is immutable. That is to say, He is unchangeable, He is forever the same! Christ is the same yesterday, today and forever (Hebrews 13:8). We must put our faith and trust in that very strong foundation. A simple statement of faith is "Jesus loves me this I know, for the Bible tells me so." It is a statement based upon the fact that God's Word is truth.

The walk of faith requires we become as a little child. Child like faith and innocence may have been stolen from you, but God can and will restore it. Part of that restoration may come as we observe children in the wonder and splendor of play. Some of our childlikeness will return as we love the unlovely child near us, who often exhibit parts of ourselves which we would like to reject or even punish. When we walk by faith we must also confess our faith. Confession of our faith means nothing more than speaking the truth about ourselves in the midst of circumstances where we normally might respond according to old patterns.

I may be suffering from illness, but to paraphrase scripture "by His stripes I am healed" (I Peter 2:24). Yes, I may be suffering from difficulties on the job. I may have trouble in my family. I may not be communicating well, but by God's grace and mercy I am an overcomer and I will overcome by faith (I John 5:1-5).

Those statements help us to live in the truth of God rather than living in that which is true only by observation of our current circumstances. Remember, because of our dysfunctional family we are not likely see the world correctly.

Our view of reality is distorted because of our past. Therefore, until we have the perfect mind of Christ, we must continue to look at things through the eyes of faith by His Word. We are going to make mistakes. When we do, we confess, we forgive, we accept responsibility, we release and we get on with our lives. We search for answers, but we live in the reality of God's Word and what God has said about us. We must learn to remind ourselves of certain truths and choose to walk in them.

All believers have been wonderfully adopted into the family of God. Because of this adoption, we have privileges - an inheritance - including the blessings of God we were robbed of because of the curses of the past. A part of this inheritance includes the reality that the Lord has given us a new name, an identity related to Father God.

God wants us to move forward in our walk of truth, to live by faith, not by sight, to live in victory and to fully possess our possessions.

God is looking for such a people as His possession. Out of the rubble of the broken lives caused by the sin of the 60's and the 70's is going to emerge a Church that will be without spot or wrinkle. The fact of the Kingdom of God is that His Kingdom will come and His will be done, on earth as it is in heaven.

Beware of despairing about yourself: you are commanded to put your trust in God, and not in yourself.

- St. Augustine -

Stan E. DeKoven, Ph.D.

Chapter Ten

Rebuilding Trust

Many counselees have expressed grave concerns about forgiveness. Their statements go something like, "If I forgive, he or she can hurt me again. I just don't want to be hurt anymore."

I too was fearful of rejection and abandonment if I opened my heart to forgive. Yet, there is a wide gap between forgiveness (commanded by the Lord; which is a process) and trust.

To trust in a thief who has not repented would be foolish. Trust must be developed, and is measured by the trustworthiness of the individual we are in a covenant relationship with. If a person, (including mom, dad, sibling, pastor) has proven to be untrustworthy with your feelings, lacks confidentiality, or is abusive, to attempt closeness would set oneself up for further pain. Therefore, small steps of self disclosure, communication and care should be shown.

The reason the writer of Proverbs could emphatically declare, *"Trust in the Lord with all your heart"* (Proverbs 3:5), was because of the unequivocal trustworthiness of God. Because of His unfailing faithfulness, we can trust Father God perfectly. He is the only one who will never fail.

A naive, childish faith, or an all-consuming perfect love in human relationships will undeniably lead to injury. No human will ever meet our criteria of perfection because perfection in this life is a myth. We must relinquish this standard for man and place our true unreserved trust in the Lord. All other trust, even with restored relationships in an earthly father, will have times of disappointment. He (and amazingly, you too) are only human.

Trust can grow as honest communication and appropriate boundaries (rules agreed to) are established and followed. Do not expect a return to the womb. God's call is to press on and forward toward the high calling of God in Christ Jesus

> *"I press toward the mark for the prize of the high calling of God in Christ Jesus,"* (Phil. 3:14).

As we press forward, we go one step at a time, putting our trust in the Lord to the best of our ability.

Hopefully by now you have a least begun your process of walking with the Holy Spirit and have formed a loving partnership through the process of Renunciation, Repentance and Restoration. The next prayer (or a similar one designed by yourself) will remind you of your continued journey of faith in God's goodness and grace.

The Prayer of Recommitment

Dear Father,

I thank You that I can come boldly before Your throne of grace to find help and mercy. I need Your mercy and grace. In so many ways I have failed to keep my covenant commitments to You and others.

Forgive me.

In light of all You have done for me, I commit myself anew, and humbly submit myself to Your Lordship. Help me to remember my commitment to fidelity and faithfulness to You, to my spouse, my children, my family, my church, my employer, my nation.

I love You, Lord, and choose to walk in Your light every day. Remind me when I fail so I can recommit daily.

Thank You Lord, in Jesus' Name, I am yours. Amen.

Living With the Scars

You never forget. You will always carry in your memory the scars of past trauma, just as you do an old wound on your body. Living with the scars is a part of living the resurrected life. For even our Lord Jesus carries in His body the scars of His crucifixion and rejection. In His hands, feet and side He continues to demonstrate His complete identification with our suffering, betrayal, and brokenness. You will always carry the scars, but Christ and His Body can help you bear the pain until your healing and restoration is complete.

Blessings and Divine Destiny

Through Christ, we are promised a divine destiny. The patterns of destruction, the areas of vulnerability, the strategy of the enemy, and our own deceptive patterns can never negate the plan and purpose of God. God's plan for good for all of His children is forever predetermined.

This divine blessing can be blocked, and that is Satan's strategy. In fact, the greater the destiny of an individual the more intense will be the attack. Thus we are urged to renounce the destructive patterns learned in our family of origin, and embrace our promised inheritance. Thus, we will with God's help, fulfill our unique place in the Body of Christ.

Stan E. DeKoven, Ph.D.

So much of what we become (males or females) depends on the role of the father image in our lives. Mothers may bring us into the world, but much of our emotions and psychological destiny is related to our relationship with the male parent.

- Joseph J. Bohac -

Stan E. DeKoven, Ph.D.

Chapter Eleven

I Want To Be Like You, Dad

Sometime after my sixth birthday, long before my "white picket fence," incident, another special event occurred. It provides a picture of father-son fundamental bonding which will allow for relationship building. There must be some bond of attachment if bridges are to be built. Fortunately, I have a few that have assisted in my restoration.

During summers in the late 1950's, long before the advent of videos, nintendo, etc., children in my neighborhood would play games requiring minor participation skills such as "Hide and Seek," "Mother May I?," and "Ring Around the Rosies." In my "hood," the favorite was "Blind Man's Bluff." For the uninformed, this game required that one person, the blind man (me in this story), try and touch one of the other children while blind-folded. The other children attempted to "bluff" the blind man, thus avoiding capture.

This particular summer night, I was "chosen" to be the blind man. Earlier that day, my mom and dad, who were quite poor, had scraped together enough money to buy me a new pair of white tennis shoes. So not only was I the blind man, but I was the best new shoes wearing blind man on the block!

As the game progressed, I could not find anyone close, so I ventured out with confidence beyond the center of the yard. I lunged for a child, hoping to be freed from my blindness, when I tripped over a sprinkler head, causing me to plunge face first onto some jagged edged bricks. I suffered a rather nasty cut on my mouth. As I staggered home, my tears mixed with blood flowing freely. I cried out for first aid and some compassion. I then looked down in dismay to see the violation of my white shoes - now blood splattered.

When I arrived at my house, my parents comforted and attended to my wounds. I kept saying to my dad, "My shoes! My shoes!" Then I asked my dad the profound existential question, "Dad, why did this have to happen to me?"

His simple response was, "Son, I don't know. Don't worry, it will be all right."

Somehow those words gave sufficient comfort and expressed the profound truth that my dad had the power, as he held me in his arms, to make everything "all right."

During the reconciling phase of our relationships, this memory provided enough foundational support to give faith for the process, and hope for the future. The Holy Spirit can and will bring you an anchor for your soul from your past, and will provide one for your relationship with your heavenly Father: Ask Him.

Knowing Him

We cannot know the Father outside of Christ. Jesus Himself said if you have seen Him, you have seen the Father (John 14:9).

If we know Him, we know the Father. Having seen and known Him, we have access directly to the Father by Jesus Christ the righteous.

> *"For through him we both have access to the Father by one Spirit,"* (Ephesians 2:18).

> *"According to his eternal purpose which he accomplished in Christ Jesus our Lord. In him and through faith in him we may approach God with freedom and confidence,"* (Ephesians 3:11-12).

Christ is our example of what it means to be in right relationship with a father, especially our Heavenly Father. In Philippians 2:7-8, we see that Christ humbled Himself - even to the point of death on the cross. For the restoration of a father/son relationship, it is necessary to humble yourself and present yourself to your Father.

In the natural, I used to think it was my father's responsibility to come to me. However, he never shut the door to our relationship. The door has always been open. I had to humble myself and come to him and present my grievances to him.

In Matthew 5 (KJV), Jesus is speaking about the attributes of the kingdom. He speaks specifically that *"blessed are the poor in spirit for theirs is the kingdom of heaven,"* (verse 3). In the 8th verse it says, *"Blessed are the pure in heart, for they shall see God."* Verse 9, states, *"Blessed are the peacemakers, for they shall be called sons of God."*

From these scriptures I came to recognize that I had no claim to holiness and superiority over my earthly father. I had to acknowledge my own poverty of spirit first. Then, I had to make sure that my heart was pure before the Lord.

The purpose of my confrontation with my father (and eventually the purpose of my coming to my Heavenly Father) was not to attempt, as Job did, to prove my righteousness. Instead it was to recognize and admit that I have no righteousness outside of Christ. Even more important, I want and need to have a relationship with my father, both earthly and heavenly.

To be called a son of God, I need to be a peacemaker. My purpose in to talking with my earthly father and my Heavenly Father was/is to bring peace in our relationship and open the door to positive communication.

I had to forgive my natural father. In some ways, even though my Heavenly Father could do no wrong, my immature attitude held that

Stan E. DeKoven, Ph.D.

God had allowed hurts to happen to me. So I also needed to "forgive" my Heavenly Father even though God the Father needs no forgiveness.

It is sometimes helpful for us to say the words, "I don't hold you further accountable for the things that have happened." Our natural fathers were attacked by the devil who had a plot against them as well as us to rob, kill and destroy. In spite of that, Jesus is still the life-giver, and He gives it more abundantly. I had to repent and let go of my anger, placing accountability on the devil, and on those who were responsible for my pain.

Yet, I could not hold them responsible in terms of blame, and allow resentment or bitterness to develop. I had to accept God's forgiveness before I could really begin the process of reestablishing the Father's love in my heart.

The Word says that God is love. I had to learn the essence of His love. His love was both a friendship, phileo-type of love, along with agape. He is unconditional love.

His grace was given to me without measure.

He poured out His love upon me at the beginning of my relationship with Him. I had tried to experience is love in the fullness measure. His love and grace, given by God is so free, yet it is very difficult when raised in dysfunctional family systems to experience it. We do not experience the love of God because, many times, we have not experienced it from our natural father. Yet, to blame the natural father will not bring restoration of that love. Truthfully, Jesus deserved all love; instead He gave love. Instead of demanding all righteousness, He gave of Himself to be the righteousness for all of mankind.

Much of our healing comes as we begin to step out of ourselves, seeking love, and begin to give that which God has given to us. This type of unselfish love is demonstrated in the tradition of

168

adoption as know in the time of the Apostle Paul. Romans 8:14-17 speaks of the spirit of adoption.

> *"Because those who are led by the Spirit of God are sons of God. For you did not receive a spirit that makes you a slave again to fear, but you receive the Spirit of sonship. And by him we cry, 'Abba, Father.' The Spirit himself testifies with our spirit that we are God's children. Now if we are children, then we are heirs – heirs of God and co-heirs with Christ, if indeed we share in his sufferings in order that we may also share in his glory."*

We have a new family and a new name! In the original Greek, the word "adoption" is "huio-thesia", which actually means "placing a son in the presence of his father." Through Christ's death and resurrection, we have been placed on the Father's lap, in His very presence. We belong to God, not just in a legal sense, but at a feeling level. The intimate relationship between ourselves and God is established through Christ and our adoption, therefore we can call Him "Abba, Daddy, Father."

As His children, we are heirs of God and joint-heirs with Christ. These facts, found in the Word of God, must be learned, accepted and received them as truth.

His love must be received by faith.

We see a beautiful picture of this adoption, this love that places us in the very presence, at a feeling level of the Father in the story of the prodigal son.

> *"Jesus continued: 'There was a man who had two sons. The younger one said to his father, 'Father, give me my share of the estate.' So he divided his property between them. Not long after that, the younger so got together all he had, set off for a distant country and then squandered his wealth in wild living. After he had spent everything,*

*there was a severe famine in that whole country, and he
began to be in need. So he went and hired himself out to
a citizen of that country, who sent him to his fields to feed
pigs. He longed to fill his stomach with the pods that the
pigs were eating, but no one gave him anything. When
he came to his senses, he said, 'How many of my father's
hired men have food to spare, and here I am starving to
death! I will set out and go back to my father and say to
him: Father, I have sinned against heaven and against
you. I am no longer worthy to be called your son; make
me like one of your hired men.' So he got up and went to
his father. But while he was still a long way off, his
father saw him and was filled with compassion for him.
The son said to him, 'Father, I have sinned against
heaven and against you. I am no longer worthy to be
called your son.' But the father said to his servants,
'Quick! Bring the best robe and put it on him. Put a ring
on his finger and sandals on his feet. Bring the fattened
calf and kill it. Let's have a feast and celebrate. For this
son of mine was dead and is alive again; he was lost and
is found.' So they began to celebrate. Meanwhile, the
older son was in the field. When he came near the house,
he heard music and dancing. So he called one of the
servants and asked him what was going on. 'Your
brother has come,' he replied, 'and your father has killed
the fattened calf because he has him back safe and
sound.' The older brother became angry and refused to
go in. So his father went out and pleaded with him. But
he answered his father, 'Look! All these years I've been
slaving for you and never disobeyed your orders. Yet
you never gave me even a young goat so I could
celebrate with my friends. But when this son of yours
who has squandered your property with prostitutes
comes home, you kill the fattened calf for him!' 'My
son,' the father said, 'you are always with me, and
everything I have is yours. But we had to celebrate and*

*be glad, because this brother of yours was dead and is
alive again; he was lost and is found,'"* (Luke 15:11-32).

In this story we see a powerful illustration of a number of things,
both in terms of an individual's life as well as a type and picture of
the Church. From the very beginning, we can see how the younger
son had the inheritance God had planned for him. This really is not
a picture of someone who is outside of Christ but one who has
received Him. He took what God gave him, the gifts, the talent, the
capabilities, and squandered them on selfish desires and scandalous
living. He became so involved in his immorality, and the waste of
his inheritance, that he ended up doing the unspeakable: slopping
pigs. Ultimately, he came to his senses and returned to his father.

Notice the attitude of the father - he welcomed him home with open
arms. He ran to him, being moved with compassion. He embraced
him, kissed him, provided for him, threw a party for him. It is
interesting to compare the father's attitude to that of the Church,
towards those in the Body of Christ who have fallen do to sin and
then return. The attitude often is, "Don't give them a second
chance." We tend to treat these sinners as the older brother did, as
though they are somehow second class in the kingdom of God.

Instead, God is saying our attitude should be one of "Quickly, let's
restore, let's rejoice that one who has been lost has been found"

> *"Brothers, if someone is caught in a sin, you who are
> spiritual should restore him gently. But watch yourself,
> or you also may be tempted. Carry each other's
> burdens, and in this way you will fulfill the law of
> Christ,"* (Galatians 6:1-2).

This type of response is what we have wanted from our natural and
Heavenly Father. What we want, more than anything, is once we
have come to ourselves and return, to be welcomed and received, to
be loved and provided for, in spite of all we have done.

Yet, most of us do not feel worthy to receive that the Father's love. Remember, God's love is not measured by our worthiness, but by the level of sacrifice of His precious son Jesus. The prodigal son is but one picture of the father's love. There are many others found in the Word of God describing His love for all of his children (We will return to the Prodigal later).

More on the Father

There are numerous references through the Word of God that give us an indication of the Father's love for us. As we come to understand what the Word says about our Father, we are able to draw nearer to Him without fear. Some of the key principles of the Father's love include:

He has provided a home, a place of safety, a place of rest. One of the primary functions of a father is to provide and protect his wife and children (John 14). Further in Luke 12:29-37, we see the divine provision given to the children of God.

> *"And do not set your heart on what you will eat or drink; do not worry about it. For the pagan world runs after all such things, and your Father knows that you need them. But seek his kingdom, and these things will be given to you as well. Do not be afraid, little flock, for your Father has been pleased to give you the kingdom. Sell your possessions and give to the poor. Provide purses for yourselves that will not wear out, a treasure in heaven that will not be exhausted, where no thief comes near and no moth destroys. For where your treasure is, there your heart will be also. Be dressed and ready for service and keep your lamps burning, like men waiting for their master to return from a wedding banquet, so that when he comes and knocks they can immediately open the door for him. It will be good for those servants whose master finds them watching when he comes. I tell*

you the truth, he will dress himself to serve, will have them recline at the table and will come and wait on them."

We have access to Him (Hebrews 7:25 and Matthew 6:6).

Father God has chosen us. Thus, we are to act the same way He does. We can actually enter into His presence with thanksgiving and praise. (Ephesians 1:4-5).

Throughout the Word of God, there are certain things fatherhood requires. God meets every characteristic.

In Malachi 2:10, God is revealed as the fatherhood of all persons. In Jeremiah 31:9 he is known as the fatherhood of Israel. In Romans 3:29 He's also the father of the Gentiles. In John 1:12-13 He's the father of every Christian who is born into His family.

A father's love should always be toward the fatherless, to those who are in great need. We are to share covenant blessings with those adopted into the family of God (Deuteronomy 14:28-29). God even provided for the very poor, leaving the gleanings at harvest time for those who are in need (Deuteronomy 24:19-22).

Fathers treat their children with honesty (Proverbs 23:10); to be prepared to defend their sons and daughters (Psalms 82:3); to visit those who are hurting and homeless (James 1:27). We are not to oppress if we are a father of the faith (Zechariah 7:10); we should show no violence toward those in need (Jeremiah 22:3).

"Though my father and mother forsake me, the LORD will receive me," (Psalms 27:10). This verse speaks very clearly that though David felt abandoned by his father, the Lord became Father to him. There is special help we can receive from God. God is The Father (Psalm 68:5), our helper (Exodus 22:22-23), and He hears our cry.

We can truly anticipate great things from our heavenly Father.

In the book of Malachi we see a powerful, prophetic word. In the last days the hearts of the fathers would be returned to the children, and of the children to the fathers, lest a curse be brought upon our land (Malachi 4:6). Many people believe a curse is already upon the land. The curse, demonstrated in the breakdown of the family (because of immorality and the hedonistic lifestyle in our world), effects the young and old, rich and poor, strong and weak.

God as our Father wants to make Himself real to His children. The process of our restoration continues with our entering into secret places, and dealing with hidden fortresses.

Prayer for the Father

Dear Lord,

I know that you are my Father, regardless of my past, no matter how I was or was not loved by my natural father (or mother). I accept you as my Father, I know you through Jesus, and I know you through your Word. Now Lord, help me to know you by experience. As I enter daily into the "secret places" with you, I know I will learn about you and become intimate with you. Help me, in the name of Jesus, your Son.

When you have closed your doors and darkened your room, remember never to say that you are alone; God is within, and your genius in within - and what need have they of light to see what you are doing?

- Epictetus: Discourses, Bk I, Ch 14 -

Stan E. DeKoven, Ph.D.

Chapter Twelve

Secret Places: Hidden Fortresses

In this last section, I would like to share some scriptures that speak about the greatness of God... His wonder, His love, and His mercy. Hopefully these words will reveal to you some of the essence of who your Father is. My prayer is that He will establish His life within you more fully.

> *"He that dwells in the secret place of the Most High shall abide under the shadow of the Almighty."* (Psalms 91:1).

The Word of God indicates there is a place of dwelling, a place of rest for us. It's a secret place, a place established by the Most High God. We as the people of God, invited to abide in Him, can actually rest under the shadow of the Almighty! In place of the hidden fortress or strongholds, God creates the secret place for us to intimately fellowship with Him.

As I remember back on the "white shoes" and my dad's comforting me, I can relate to the "secret place" of safety. The white picket fence incident created a broken place that became a stronghold which the devil hoped would seal my heart from the Father. Yet the Father's love was and is more powerful than the strongest stronghold.

We need to receive a revelation, an unveiling of the Father and His love and purpose for the Church! The word "revelation" ("apocalypsis" in the Greek) means "to uncover or unveil." From the beginning, the Father has wanted to unveil Himself. So much has the Father desired this that He gave to us His Son as the express image of His divine intention for our lives (Hebrews 1, John 1, Ephesians 1). We enter into the place of rest, understanding the nurturing and love of God and His protection as we dwell in the secret place. Psalms 27:5 says,

> *"For in the day of trouble he will keep me safe in his dwelling; he will hide me in the shelter of his tabernacle and set me high upon a rock,"* (Psalm 27:5).

God understands the troubles. His promise, if we will listen to it and heed His voice, states that He will bring us into His pavilion, into His secret tabernacle hidden with Him and established on His rock of safety.

> *"In the shelter of your presence you hide them from the intrigues of men; in your dwelling you keep them safe from accusing tongues,"* (Psalms 31:20).

What a beautiful picture of the protection and love of the Lord!

> *"You are my hiding place; you will protect me from trouble and surround me with songs of deliverance. Selah,"* (Psalm 32:7. See also Psalm 9:9 and Exodus 15:1-21).

There is a song of deliverance!

There is a place where we can sing unto the Lord the new song, a song of deliverance, the shout of joy because we know He will preserve us in the most difficult times.

> *"Keep me as the apple of thine eye, hid me in the shadow of they wings,"* (Psalms 17:8, KJV).

I often think about my own children, especially when they were first born, there will always be something very special in my heart. What a tremendous sense of joy, accomplishment and meaning. Having children and being a father means so much to me. I can only approximate the sense of joy our Father in Heaven must have in us.

In Matthew 6:6 we see a key to how this special relationship with the father is developed. It reads,

> *"But when you pray, go into your room, close the door and pray to your Father, who is unseen. Then your Father, who sees what is done in secret, will reward you."*

This passage reminds me of the story in II Kings 4:33 of Elisha and the Shunamite woman when Elisha raised her son from the dead. The woman in the story understood so well that because of her love, care and support of the prophet, she was in the position to receive what was needed for her life, at her time of need. Her relationship with the prophet went far beyond just acknowledging him as a man of God.

They had a special relationship of mutual respect. She ministered to him, and when it was her time of need, he ministered to her - not out of obligation, but out of love, mutual respect and honor that they had for each other.

When we enter into the secret place, closing ourselves off from the world and its distractions, we set ourselves aside to enter into the holy presence of God. Our Lord, who sees in secret (the secret place, alone with Him) will reward us openly.

But first, it says to go to your room. There is a special place for all of us where we can commune with the Lord in a time of intimacy. It is a physical place and a spiritual place. For me, my best time is usually after 8 o'clock at night when I take a walk. There is nobody around and it is quiet. And as I walk, I am able to commune with the Lord in a precious harmony. The secret place does not have to be a literal room, but it is a place where you can close yourself in with God.

Second, we are told to close our door. The shutting of the door is a determination, a decision to allow the Lord in your presence and to wait in the presence of the Lord. To shut your door is to close off distractions. Our temptation, as we strive to make ends meet, provide for our family, and function in ministry, is to forget about our most important relationship; that special relationship with our Father God. To be able to separate oneself, to shut the door to any outside activity is vitally important.

Third, the Bible says to pray to the Father. Most people pray to Jesus, and there is certainly nothing wrong with that. Jesus stated, "I want to show you the Father." He wanted to introduce us to His Father who is in the secret place. As we pray in that quiet place and enter into the presence of God, God communes with us, and we commune with Him. The Father sees in secret. As we open ourselves to Him, He sees the secret desires of our heart and the secret sins we confess and He forgets.

He openly rewards our secret desires. Why? Because of the reciprocal relationship that has developed between us and the Father. The Father's love is beyond true description. He is waiting for His children to enter into their place of rest, in the presence of the Father, to thoroughly enjoy the status of their adoption. He desires His children to enter into that secret place and to commune with the Father.

We were made for fellowship with the Father! We were made to share our deepest secrets with Him!

This is neither a grievous thing nor frightening to an adopted child. They are fully received and accepted. They are welcome in the presence of the Father. The Lord desires that relationship with us, and as we develop that relationship, we begin to move forward in reestablishing the father image within ourselves.

Many clients have expressed intense fear of this level of intimacy. This comes from the reality that deep intimacy, for most, has never been experienced. However, when one begins with a Godly image in their sanctified mind, using our imagination as God intended, we can slowly gain a greater sense of confidence in the Lord and His goodness. His mercy is forever to His children who are walking in the righteousness provided by Christ.

Prayer, praise and worship in the secret place set the stage for a deep healing and satisfying relationship. It begins as we allow our sanctified imagination to picture ourselves in the Father's arms, or under the shadow of His wings, or in the cleft of the Rock. Picture your place of safety where only you and your Father commune and take time every day to rest there. As you do, you will begin to receive the revelation of God's love and establish the place of safety in Him needed to launch your walk in the Lord.

A Final Picture: Lazarus

A final picture of God's plan for deliverance and restoration is illustrated in the biblical story of the death and resurrection of Lazarus. The story, recorded in John 11: 1-44 begins;

> *"Now a man name Lazarus was sick. He was from Bethany, the village of Mary and her sister Martha. This Mary, whose brother Lazarus now lay sick, was the same one who poured perfume on the Lord and wiped his feet with her hair. So the sisters sent word to Jesus, 'Lord, the one you love is sick.' When he heard this, Jesus said, 'This sickness will not end in death. No, it is for God's glory so that God's Son may be glorified through it.' Jesus loved Martha and her sister and Lazarus. Yet when he heard that Lazarus was sick, he stayed where he was two more days. Then he said to his disciples, 'Let us go back to Judea.' 'But Rabbi,' they said, 'a short while ago the Jews tried to stone you, and yet you are going back there?' Jesus answered, 'Are there not twelve hours of daylight? A man who walks by day will not stumble, for he sees by this world's light. It is when he walks by night that he stumbles, for he has no light.' After he had said this, he went on to tell them, 'Our*

friend Lazarus has fallen asleep; but I am going there to wake him up.' His disciples replied, 'Lord, if he sleeps, he will get better.' Jesus had been speaking of his death, but his disciples thought he meant natural sleep. So then he told them plainly, 'Lazarus is dead, and for your sake I am glad I was not there, so that you may believe. But let us go to him.' Then Thomas (called Didymus) said to the rest of the disciples, 'Let us also go, that we may die with him.' On his arrival, Jesus found that Lazarus had already been in the tomb for four days. Bethany was less than two miles from Jerusalem, and many Jews had come to Martha and Mary to comfort them in the loss of their brother. When Martha heard that Jesus was coming, she went out to meet him, but Mary stated at home. 'Lord,' Martha said to Jesus, 'if you had been here, my brother would not have died. But I know that even now God will give you whatever you ask.' Jesus said to her, 'Your brother will rise again.' Martha answered, ' I know he will rise again in the resurrection at the last day.' Jesus said to her, 'I am the resurrection and the life. He who believes in me will live, even though he dies; and whoever lives and believes in me will never die. Do you believe this?' 'Yes, Lord,' she told him, 'I believe that you are the Christ, the Son of God, who was to come into the world.' And after she had said this, she went back and called her sister Mary aside. 'The Teacher is here,' she said, 'and is asking for you.' When Mary heard this, she got up quickly and went to him. Now Jesus had not yet entered the village, but was still at the place where Martha had met him. When the Jews who had been with Mary in the house, comforting her, noticed how quickly she got up and went out, they followed her, supposing she was going to the tomb to mourn there. When Mary reached the place where Jesus was and saw him, she fell at his feet and said, 'Lord, if you had been here, my brother would not have died.' When Jesus saw her weeping, and the Jews who had come along with her also weeping, he was deeply moved in spirit and troubled. 'Where have you laid him?' he asked. 'Come and see, Lord,' they replied. Jesus wept. Then the Hews said, 'See how he loved him!' But some of them said, 'Could not he who opened the eyes of the blind man have kept this man from dying?' Jesus, once more deeply moved, came to the tomb. It was a cave with a stone laid across the entrance. 'Take away the stone,' he said. 'But, Lord,' said Martha, the sister of the dead man, 'by this time there is a bad odor, for he has been there four days.' Then Jesus said, 'Did I not tell you that if you believed, you would see the glory of the God?' So they took away the stone. Then Jesus looked up and said, 'Father, I thank you that you have heard me. I knew that you always hear me, but I said this for the benefit of the people standing here, that they may believe that you sent me.' When he had said this, Jesus called in a loud voice, 'Lazarus, come out!' The dead man came out, his hands and feet wrapped with strips of linen, a cloth around his face. Jesus said to them, 'Take off the grace clothes and let him go.'"

In the 10th chapter of John, Jesus asserts His deity through His teaching and the demonstration of His power. As His renown spread, the Pharisees and Sadducees tried to discredit him; the desire by the populace to crown Him king was mounting. In the midst of this inevitable confrontation, the news of Lazarus came to Jesus. Lazarus was the brother of Mary and Martha, and a friend of Jesus.

Jesus knew all along of the condition of Lazarus, and his impending death. Though Jesus was frequently moved with compassion to quickly alleviate suffering and provide healing, He delayed his travel to Bethany due to the life over death encounter He would face.

His disciples did not understand the purpose of Jesus' statement in John 11:15, nor His plan for Lazarus. Their assumption was that Jesus was going to die, and they were morbidly following Him. (It is often true that we, as God's servants, are unaware of the Lord, His plans or power.) Yet, they did obediently follow Christ.

In the 17th verse, Jesus speaks to Martha and proclaims to her a powerful and revolutionary statement. Jesus said, *"I am the resurrection and the life"* (Vs 25). Her understanding of that statement is similar to many today... that the resurrection Jesus was speaking was a future "sweet by and by" time.

However, Jesus was speaking in the ever present now. "I AM that I AM is here, and I am the resurrection. I am the life." Martha had faith to believe for the future, for the eventual, but did not or could not believe for the now. (More will be said on this later.)

Shortly thereafter, He encountered Mary, the one who ministered to Jesus. She made the same statement as his sister, Martha. They both knew that Jesus could have prevented the death of Lazarus. Yet, her statement apparently was filled with faith, expectancy and experiential belief. Jesus did not need to explain to her about the resurrection.

Mary knew Jesus as the resurrection. She had experienced His power of deliverance, her own personal resurrection. He only asked where Lazarus was buried.

Perhaps Mary's faith, and later her expression of grief and mourning (Vs. 33), is what moved Him to tears and troubled His spirit. This will occur in men and women of God when God the Holy Spirit is preparing to move in great power through us. Our emotions can become overwhelmed as our spirit is troubled.

In the 38th verse, the cave in which Lazarus was entombed is briefly described. As was the tradition of the day, holes were dug out of a hillside, and a place was prepared for the deceased, and eventually, the entire family. A very heavy stone was rolled in front of the grave, provided for sanctity and protection for the dead, as well as for future access.

From the 38th verse through the 44th, the incredibly powerful encounter and victory of Christ over death is presented, resulting in the conspiracy to have the Lord Jesus put to death. I will provide commentary on verses 38-44 from a counseling ministry perspective. Along with commentary I will illustrate God's plan for our total redemption with an application to the restoration of the father image.

First of all, nothing the Lord did on earth was by accident. Not only was everything planned, but all was planned for our example. Jesus was moved deeply with compassion for Mary and Martha, but also with the knowledge of what was soon to occur. Rather than commanding the stone to move from its place (within His power), He solicited the help of people who cared for Lazarus.

Martha speaks a word of intellectual reason, rooted in her reality. Because of the length of time Lazarus had been dead, his body would have begun to decompose, emitting a distinctly foul odor. Jesus again reinforced to her what she could not see. Mary does not speak. Perhaps she already knew that nothing was impossible with God.

The story of Lazarus is frequently presented as an illustration of the transformation of an unbeliever. Yet, Lazarus was not an unbeliever. He both believed in and followed Christ. The cave provides an illustration of the life of a believer. Jesus' ministry demonstrates God's powerful deliverance from hidden fortresses which are contained in dark places.

A cave is a dark, damp, isolated place that has no life within. However, from the outside, all anyone can see is the rock covering something. Only someone who had gazed behind the rock could state authoritatively what was hidden there. If you will, this cave illustrates a dark, hidden place, a place of death or brokenness, covered by a heavy defense mechanism to protect the contents inside.

The command of the Lord to those who care (caregivers, not psychological voyeurs) is to remove the stone. It is essential for the defensive mask people wear to be lovingly removed if we are to minister to the true need.

Also, note the reality statement made by Martha, "he stinketh!" When you or I begin to see behind the masks, behind the stones, the story presented will likely stink. However, if you are to care for others or be cared for by others, you must be able to stand the stench in people's hearts.

Jesus was neither discouraged nor embarrassed by the reality of humanity. Jesus was not fearful of becoming stinky by association.

Jesus' prayer is most interesting. He prayed for those who were listening. Jesus was "prayed up" and did not need to do a religious activity. However, he wanted those around him to be fully aware that it is Christ who has the power to command death unto life.

A counselor, pastor or a friend helps you see behind your mask, removing the stone. You may be one who assists others who are in a hidden fortress of darkness where "stinking thinking" exists. Yet, we must always remember that it is the power of God that brings deliverance, not our skill or our goodness. Only God deserves glory. Jesus called Lazarus forth!

When Lazarus came hopping out of the tomb, he did so completely bound with grave clothes. What a picture of those Christ has called from death unto life. He/we came from our hidden fortress with the stinky clothes (attitude, beliefs, feelings, fears, etc.) that he/we had within the cave. He was fully alive, but was unable to function.

Death and its bondage created his dysfunction (apparently viewed as normal by Jesus), and Jesus could have commanded the bindings to fall off of Lazarus. However, Jesus commands those who love Lazarus to unbind him and set him at liberty. Notice the bindings. Lazarus came from the grave bound hand, foot, and across the face.

Lazarus was bound in his hands... the hands are used to grab, to touch, to hold, to communicate with. Without hands we are unable to function well; our ability to care for our own needs is extremely limited. Lazarus was alive but unable to even feed himself without the help of others.

Lazarus was bound about the feet... this would limit his basic sense of balance, making him most vulnerable. He could be easily tripped or knocked off center. He would not have the ability to motor himself, act on his own, determine by his own will. He did not have the ability to or move in the direction of choice.

Lazarus was bound about the face... he had eyes, but could not see. He had ears, but could not hear. He had a mouth, but could not speak.

The Lord Jesus Christ has every intention for all humanity to be alive and fully functional. We must allow God to deliver us. To do so, we must have the stones removed so that the light of God's Word can flood into the darkness in our hearts, so the love of God can transform us.

Further, we must allow the Body of Christ to assist us unwrapping, liberating us through loving care. We then can see, hear, speak, touch, and move according to God's perfect plan for our lives. This is a process that takes time, but is available to all, no matter how "dead" or seemingly destroyed we are by the world, or sin.

Stan E. DeKoven, Ph.D.

Naught but God
Can satisfy the soul

- Philip James Bailey: Festus: Heaven -

Stan E. DeKoven, Ph.D.

Chapter Thirteen

Father God:
Rebuilding a Godly Self-Concept

Many have misbeliefs about the character of God that originate from their family or church background, or from injustices they have received from others. This is a major underlying factor in most acting-out behavior. Restoration requires an understanding of God and His character. In the heart of the individual, the revelation of the Father as demonstrated in Jesus Christ must be experienced.

Dr. Bruce Litchfield, in his doctoral thesis on *Sexual Dysfunction* (1990), writes... *"The Old Testament gives many revelations (declarations) of who God is. While the Old Testament does not give us the fullness of the revelation of God known as Father, it nevertheless gives many helpful insights about God's character."*

For instance, the 19th Psalm provides a revelation of God's Glory as seen in creation. *"The heavens declare the glory of God..."* and also of His law, verse 7 states:

> *"The law of the LORD is perfect, reviving the soul. The statutes of the LORD are trustworthy, making wise the simple. The precepts of the LORD are right, giving joy to the heart. The commands of the LORD are radiant, giving light to the eyes. The fear of the LORD is pure, enduring forever. The ordinances of the LORD are sure and altogether righteous,"* (Psalm 19:7-9).

David, convicted of his sin states in verse 12, *"Forgive my hidden faults. Keep your servant also from willful sins..."*

In Psalm 139 we see the nature of God in His omniscience, omnipotence, omnipresence, and omnipersonal ways with us, especially in the individual formation of each of us.

Thus David prays in verse 23,

> *"Search me, O God, and know my heart; test me and know my anxious thoughts."*

Probably the most important aspect of the character of God is His holiness - the summation of all His attributes.

In the Old Testament are pictures of God's awesomeness. Our most complete picture of God as Father comes through the relationship between Father God and Jesus. Again, Dr. Litchfield states...

> *"No one has ever seen God, but God the One and Only, who is at the Father's side, has made him known,"* (John 1:18).

> *"Nor does anyone know the Father except the Son, and he to whom the Son wills to reveal Him,"* (Matthew 11:27b, KJV).

Jesus came as an extension of the love of the Father. Mankind, hopelessly lost in insufferable futility, needed one who could show the way to life.

> *"God so loved the world that He gave His only begotten Son that whosoever believes on Him should not perish but have eternal life"* (John 3:16, KJV).

God the Father loves, He gives, and He wants us to experience abundant life eternally.

What is eternal life? Jesus exclaims, while praying to His Father,

> *"Now this is eternal life: that they may know you, the only true God, and Jesus Christ, whom you have sent,"* (John 17:3).

Throughout John's Gospel, Jesus goes to great lengths to make the Father known, and show us the way to Him. If that was truly the plan of the Father, then why do so many have trouble with the Father image? Jesus' objective was to show us the Father by demonstrating His love for us through His sacrificial death and resurrection.

Because of misconceptions of God as Father, we mostly relate to Jesus, speaking, praying, and even longing for Him. Yet Jesus said, *"He who has seen Me has seen the Father"* and that He is *"the way, the truth and the life; no one can come to the Father except by Me"* (John 14:6), and that *"I and My Father are one"* (John 10:30). Jesus prays to His Father,

> *"I have declared to them Your name and will declare it, that the love with which You have love Me may be in them and I in them"* (John 17:26).

Jesus also prayed to the Father, and it is part of our pattern prayer saying, *"Our Father in heaven, hallowed be Your name."* (Luke 11:2)

A primary goal of Christ was to model for mankind a most intimate and wonderfully personal relationship with the Father. For mankind to experience this relationship, they must learn to enter into the presence of the Lord. As Christians, we do not have to be timid in doing so, as the apostle states, *"Through Him (Christ) we both (Jew and Gentile) have access by one Spirit to the Father"* (Ephesians 2:18), and *"Having therefore, brethren, boldness to enter into the holiest by the blood of Jesus,"* (Hebrews 10:19). To enter into the presence of the Father is to set aside our own agenda, to close off all distractions, and focus our attention on our great and mighty God.

Certainly He is Abba (Daddy) Father, but He is also awesome, all powerful, and to be reverenced above all things.

Entering into God's presence takes commitment and practice, and leads to the intimacy we so desperately need and deserve. The practice of entering into His presence daily is the secret ingredient to every great spiritual leader's power for effective living.

Finally, Dr. Litchfield mentions that as we come into the presence of God, we experience six things, among others, which I call "The Six A's." They are:

1. Acceptance

> John 1:12 states *"Yet to all who received him, to those who believed in his name, he gave the right to become children of God"* - He accepts us for who we are as created in His image, but also as His children and His sons. Acceptance was one of the things that I longed for with my natural father. I felt so unacceptable because I knew that I would "never amount to nothing". Though my adult mind could accept that my natural father's words were not based upon truth, my heart had fully embraced the lie. Only through the work of the cross in my life and my eventual trust in the Father's love opened the door to God's acceptance.

2. Affirmation

> He affirms us and establishes our true identity. In John 1:42 it says of Peter, *"And he (Andrew) brought him to Jesus. Now, when Jesus looked at him, He said, You are Simon the son of Jonah, You shall be called Cephas (a stone)."* In another place, Jesus affirms His disciples (Luke 22:28-30). As we come into the presence of Jesus, we find that He leads us into the Father's presence. This is where we learn the perfection of fatherhood - the father heart of God. Often we need to experience this affirmation from others of influence in the Body of Christ. Finding men and women of Godly character who can and will with delight affirm our significance in life is a search well worth our effort.

3. Affection

In His presence we prove the reality of the love of Christ, *"to know the love of Christ which surpasses knowledge"* (Ephesians 3:19), and the love of God, the Father. *"The Father Himself has affection for you, because you have had affection for Me and believed that I came out from God"* (John 16:27). Jesus prayed to His Father, *"that the love which You have loved Me may be in them and I in them"* (John 17:26).

Affection without exploitation is essential for our ultimate healing and restoration. We know that the Lord will not hurt us, but what about others in the church. The fact is, many hurting people in the church continue to look for victims to further exploit for their own purposes. Thus, we must use great wisdom in selecting the relationships we choose. This wisdom comes through the multitude of counselors, or mature believers that lack a hidden agenda. Since our ability to make good choices has been impaired from past encounters, it is necessary to find positive models to follow. Generally, a loving Pastor or Elder in a local church is a good place to start to find the affection we need. All I really know is that the search is worth the effort, and God will provide to us the affection we need through the members in the Body of Christ where he has placed us. We must not give up the search.

4. Approval

Paul told Timothy to *"Be diligent to present yourself approved to God, a worker who does not need to be ashamed"* (2 Timothy 2:15). God delights to indicate His approval to His servants who faithfully serve Him. Jesus approved the disciples even after they were at rivalry amongst themselves as to who was the greatest. After instructing them He said, *"But you are those who have continued with Me in My trials, and I bestow upon you a kingdom just as My Father bestowed one on Me."* (Luke 22:24-30). Though you may still desire to be approved by your primary caregiver, this level of approval was only to be temporary. The ultimate goal of parenting is to prepare one's children for adult, mature relationships, and to eventually turn the children over to the care of the Lord Himself. Whether our parents were wicked or wonderful, the Lord has provided His seal of approval by providing to us the Holy Spirit through our confession of faith. If God approves of us (our core self, not necessarily everything we say and do), then the opinion of man has lesser meaning.

5. Adoration

Adoration must occur as we enter God's almighty and majestic Presence. The Father is seeking worshippers (John 4:20-24). This is one of the reasons why Jesus came, to seek worshippers for the Father. Much of my early life was spent trying to repair my internal wounds and find others who could love this unlovely creature. However, this morbid and intense search for my own fulfillment lead to self absorbed preoccupation and a continued cycle of hopelessness and despair. When I began to seek the Kingdom of God first, His righteousness, when God became God and I took my rightful position under the Lordship of Christ, my perspective, purpose, and problems shifted. I began to focus on the most important thing of all, learning to love God and in turn learning to be receptive to His love. God is the only one deserving of our true and total devotion, not mom, dad, spouse or child. As such, when we worship and adore the Lord, we are no longer thinking selfishly, but are able to actually receive the benefits of a proper relationship with God. God delights and dwells in the praises of His people (Psalm 22:3). God delights in us as we delight in Him. A mutual admiration society.

6. Adjustment

God's presence is characterized by perfect love and holiness. As we approach the Lord in His love and holiness, it often necessitates spiritual adjustment on our part as to align ourselves with all that is in accord with His presence. There is no room for unbelief and pride. The lies of negativism that the enemy has whispered in our ears over the years must give way to the Word of the Lord. As we meditate on the Word of God, and as we in obedience act on that word, God begins to adjust our attitudes and beliefs. This is a process that takes time, and the Lord is rich in mercy and patience. Thank the Lord.

Even though prayer has been given, breaking past bondages, repenting of misbeliefs, restoring healthy relationships and recommitting ourselves to Christ and His plan, we must daily walk in our liberty. To do this, we must appropriate God's Word into our lives, Psalms 119:11 says, *"Thy word have I treasured (hid, KJV) in my heart, that I may not sin against thee."*

More than just reading, we must treasure God's Word. Treasuring comes by acting on God's Word, by becoming a doer of righteousness (Sanford & Sanford, Renewal of the Mind, p. 202). Daily we must allow the Word to filter down from our heads into our hearts, until our hearts become pure as our minds are renewed.

Knowing the Father's Character

The character of a natural father can run the gamut from the ridiculous to the sublime. The father we were raised with had a character mixed with the image of God and the sinfulness of His creation. However, it is not that way with our Father God. The scriptures are filled with evidence of the unique and wonderful character of God.

The following represent only some of those scriptures:

1. Favor

"Then you will win favor and a good name in the sight of God and man," (Proverbs 3:4)

God delights to show his favor to those who keep His Word.

2. Oneness

"Know therefore that the LORD your God is God; he is the faithful God, keeping his covenant of love to a thousand generations of those who love him and keep his commands," (Deuteronomy 6:4-5).

3. Faithfulness

"Know therefore that the LORD your God is God; he is the faithful God, keeping his covenant of love to a thousand generations of those who love him and keep his commands," (Deuteronomy 7:9).

"A maskil of Ethan the Ezrahite. I will sing of the Lord's great love forever; with my mouth I will make your faithfulness know thorough all generations," (Psalm 89:1).

4. Goodness

"The LORD loves righteousness and justice; the earth is full of his unfailing love," (Psalm 33:5).

5. Power

"But Jesus beheld them, and said unto them, With men this is impossible; but with God all things are possible," (Matthew 19:26).

6. Grace

"For by grace are ye saved through faith; and that not of yourselves: it is a gift of God; Not of works, lest any man should boast," (Ephesians 2:8-9).

7. Mercy

"But the mercy of the Lord is from everlasting to everlasting upon them that fear him and his righteousness unto children's children," (Psalm 103:17).

8. Love

"For God so loved the world, that he gave his only begotten Son, that whosoever believeth in him should not perish, but have everlasting life," (John 3:16).

"And we have known and believed the love that God hath to us. God is love; and he that dwelleth in love dwelleth in God, and God in him," (I John 4:16).

9. Light

"The Lord is my light and my salvation; whom shall I fear? The Lord is the strength of my life; of whom shall I be afraid?," (Psalm 27:1).

"This then is the message which we have heard of him, and declare unto you, that God is light, and in Him there is no darkness at all," (I John 1:5).

10. Knowing

"Great is our Lord, and of great power: his understanding is infinite," (Psalm 147:5).

"Neither is there any creature that is not manifest in his sight: but all things are naked and opened unto the eyes of him with whom we have to do," (Hebrews 4:13).

11. Sovereignty

"For the Lord most high is terrible; his is a great King over all the earth," (Psalm 47:2).

12. Shepherd

"So we thy people and sheep of thy pasture will give thee thanks for ever: we will shew forth thy praise to all generations," (Psalms 79:13).

Psalm 23 - The entire psalm.

13. Holy

"Who is like unto thee, O Lord, among the gods? Who is like thee, glorious in holiness, fearful in praises, doing wonders?" (Exodus 15:11).

"And one cried unto another and said, 'Holy, holy, holy, is the Lord of Hosts: the whole earth is full of his glory.'" (Isaiah 6:3).

14. Truth

"God forbid: yea, let God be true, but every man a liar; as it is written, That thou mightest be justified in thy sayings, and mightest overcome when thou art judged." (Romans 3:4).

The importance of this list of attributes is to simply state that there is noting to fear in relationship to the Father. In Christ, we have the wonderful opportunity to have a relationship with the God of the universe, and can do so without fear of rejection or abandonment. He loves us and desires relationship, just the way we are.

Accepting His Love

In our society it is difficult for men to express affectionate love. It is one of the anomalies of our world that you might be labeled as something undesirable if you show an excessive amount of affection, one male to another. Men, especially, have a difficulty communicating feelings. We have been taught, "Don't think, don't feel, don't trust, and don't be intimate." It is a part of our western culture not to show tender feelings.

I remember the first time I went to Africa. I was greeted at the airport by a pastor in Cameroon, Western Africa. When we walked out of the terminal, he took my hand. I did not know what was going on, but I learned to adapt. As we were walking down the street people did not seem to mind or really notice, other than to recognize and acknowledge that we were together. I asked him later what the hand holding meant. He said, "Well, doesn't everyone hold hands in America? All friends hold hands when they walk together in Africa."

It is very "normal" in many cultures to greet each other with a kiss on the cheek, or a hug. In our Western society, the expression of affection is rarely seen, but it is so desperately needed.

Because of the lack of bonding that often occurs with the natural father, because of our homophobic fear of being close to one another, it is essential that we break through the emotional barriers and begin to reestablish relationships man to man. We have recently seen in American society a renewed emphasis on male bonding, returning of our masculine self. Men are heading to the wood to howl at the moon or to the gym to hail one's strength in an attempt to reconnect with the core self.

That is the world's view of it.

God's plan is to restore the Father image in Church. It is in the Body of Christ, as we learn to express our feelings of love and appreciation for one another that we begin to grow in relationship and intimacy. Through relationships established in the local church we can learn to express and overcome some of the fears we have learned from childhood. The overcoming of fear, of closeness and intimacy needs to be modeled from the pulpit and through relationships in pastoral ministry.

To truly experience an intimate level of relationship with the Father, as with any other area of life, we must be willing to receive it by faith. Intimacy does not happen by chance or even specifically by design. It must first be received by faith, that is, we must begin to see ourselves as close, intimate, loved and cared for by the Father, and within the Body of Christ, in and through our sanctified imagination. To do so, we must change our present thinking. With the help of friends and the Holy Spirit, we can overcome the dysfunctional thought patterns caused by the father of lies (John 8:44).

Satan will try to rob, steal and destroy to keep us from experiencing intimacy with the Father. He knows it is within the secret place that we find God's power. At the moment that we fully realize that we are loved and accepted as new creations in Christ, we become dangerous to the kingdom of darkness.

Back To the Prodigal

We have already discussed the beautiful picture of the prodigal son. In that typological picture we see one who already had the inheritance take and squander it, living a life of immorality. We observed the process of repentance which occurred after the event, when he came to himself.

To continue with the Prodigal example, *"But when he came to his senses, he said..."* (Luke 15:17a). He became aware of his situation as it really was. For most young men and women who have been raised in a dysfunctional family system, the most difficult thing for them to do is to face the truth about who they are and what they have become. It is difficult for all of us to recognize that though God has given us a great and immeasurable inheritance, we may have squandered it.

We may not be living according to God's perfect intentions for us. It is a important to note that simple awareness is not enough. The Prodigal may have been aware of the situation he was in and chose to remain there without making a decision to change. But in verses 17b-18, KJV says,

> *"How many of my father's men have more than enough bread, but I am dying here with hunger. I will arise and go to my father."*

After we become aware of the difficulties or dysfunctions of our existence, we must then make a decision of our will to do something about it. Many people have had their wills disabled through years of abuse or denial, making it extremely difficult for them to make a decision to move forward toward health. But the decision must be made.

When it was time for my discussion with my earthly father, it was a very trepidations event. I was quite frightened that he would reject me or see me as "silly". I knew I had to talk with him, to make things right. I knew I had to make the step.

You see, no matter how great the father's love, when there has been a breach in that relationship, regardless of what caused it, it is nearly always the lesser that makes the step towards the greater. As long as there is a father and a son or father and daughter relationship, the father will always be seen as the greater. That is inevitable, and is unlikely to change.

Though we strive to be peers, I doubt if we ever achieve it. It was essential that the young man recognize he had to go to his father, that he had to make things right. In this case, the father, a type of

God the father, was righteous. He was right, and he was in a position to bring restoration or judgment. The son had made the wrong choices.

Ultimately, no matter how hard we look for who is to blame, the reality is, all we can do is take responsibility for the choices we have made and bring correction to them. A part of the son's statement in verses 18 and 19 is

> *"Father I have sinned against Heaven and in your sight. I am no longer worthy to be called your son. Make me as one of your hired men."*

That is an obvious statement of humility, a willingness to do whatever it takes to reestablish a relationship. Not just because of the great physical hunger the young man experienced, but because of his desire to return to the loving graces of the father.

Anyone raised in difficult family situations, regardless of what has happened, will continue to desire to be back in right relationship. Some cases are irreparable, especially when there has been severe physical or sexual abuse, total neglect, and no willingness to acknowledge or repent on the part of the parent. The best we can hope for perhaps is to live at peace. All we can do, and all that is required, is take it to our Heavenly Father and leave it with Him.

He is more than able to bear the burden since we cannot carry it. This is a prime reason for Christ's death and resurrection. Yet, in Galatians 6:2, it says that we are to *"bare one another's burdens."* Also, verse 4 states that in some cases there are burdens that we must bear alone.

Not only did the prodigal son decide to change, by a determination of his will, but he actually did what he determined to do. I have counseled with hundreds of people over the years who have come to an awareness of their need, who have even made clear and profound decisions. Unfortunately, they never followed through with their decision. This step must occur!

There must be a willingness to go, hat in hand, acknowledging our part of the breach in the relationship. To be willing to humble ourselves and meekly to go before our natural father as well as our heavenly Father is a vital step.

Verse 20 says that

> *"He got up and came to his father. While he was still a long way off, his father saw him and felt compassion for him and ran and embraced him and kissed him."*

The rest of the story tells about the great celebration that occurred because of the father's consuming compassion and desire to have a restored relationship with his son.

There is something truly miraculous that occurs when the barriers are broken down and the love relationship is reestablished between a father and a son or a daughter and father. Of course, the removal of barriers is not always realistic.

Often times the father will not be willing to embrace. The father will not be moved with compassion in the natural level. Even if they are, the relationship will never be perfect because perfect people do not exist. Therefore, there will always be the need to bring before both the natural father and our Heavenly Father the issues, hurts, and problems of the past. Jesus is more than willing to hear our confession. He desires to receive our repentance, and thus provide washing and cleansing, release from the sins of the past, and provide restoration to the full that inheritance which we are to possess as born again Christians. There is the "welcome home" for which all of us are looking.

Although we may never return as adults to our family of origin and become a child again, there is ever a desire for a "welcome home." It is rarely if ever possible for us to experience that full and complete welcome that we desire. We seek a feeling, sense of absolute safety, warmth and love. We so desperately wanted and needed this as children, yet it evades us still. Perhaps that is the way it's supposed to be.

If I read the scriptures correctly, there is something greater then any earthly family, something greater then any earthly accomplishment, and that is to be with the Heavenly Father.

The scriptures say Jesus came specifically to show us the Father, not a natural, earthly father, but a Heavenly Father. In His description of Him, He states that our spiritual Father, the Father of all light, has made absolute provision for us.

In John 14, Jesus speaks about a house He is going to prepare for us, assuring us that we do not have to carry a troubled heart. No matter how difficult or dysfunctional our families have been, no matter how problematic our present life is, we can look forward to a new reality. Not just a dream, not a delusion, not denial, but the reality that Jesus has gone before us and has done so to prepare a place in His father's house.

There is also a house, a home, a family that God has provided that begins here on planet Earth: the precious body of Christ. It is in the local church where all broken relationships are to be restored, healed and developed. This is a process, not an event, and not every local church is geared in the direction of restoration and healing. However, in every city there will be a church of the locality that will have the heart and resources to assist you in your healing process. God's plan always has been and always will be our restoration. Not just in the sweet bye and bye of heaven, but here on earth as members of His Kingdom.

God has provided to us a portion of all the good things necessary for us to survive and function well, both here on Earth as well in the Heavenly places. A part of that provision of being in the Father's house is found in prayer.

As we learn how to enter into the secret place, as we abide where God dwells, in our inner sanctuary, we do so with understanding and in the spirit. Under the shadow of His wing, we abide through prayer. Through praise and petition we give Him opportunity to love. We grow through meditation in His Word and by allowing ourselves to hear and receive what God would say to us. Thus, we grow into His image.

> *"Therefore, as God's chosen people, holy and dearly loved, clothe yourselves with compassion, kindness, humility, gentleness and patience. Bear with each other and forgive whatever grievances you may have against one another. Forgive as the Lord forgave you. And over all these virtues put on love, which binds them all together in perfect unity. Let the peace of Christ rule in your hearts, since as members of one body you were called to peace. And be thankful. Let the word of Christ dwell in you richly as you teach and admonish one another with all wisdom, and as you sing psalms, hymns and spiritual songs with gratitude in your hearts to God. And whatever you do, whether in word or deed, do it all in the name of the Lord Jesus, giving thanks to God the Father through him,"* (Colossians 3:12-17).

We have been chosen of God, regardless of where we were raised or what family we were born into, if we know the Lord Jesus Christ as our personal Lord and Savior. God says we are holy and beloved. Because we are holy and beloved, we can put on a heart of deep love, love in action, kindness and humility, gentleness and patience. These are characteristics not common to members of dysfunctional families, but common to members of God's family.

As I think about my father, he did not have many of these positive biblical characteristics. He had many good ones, but lacked compassion, gentleness and patience when he was young. I picked up many of those traits, and so will my children.

I have had difficulty at times with humility and patience. Yet, because of Jesus Christ, and the Holy Spirit in my life, I can choose to put on Godly characteristics. The Father is rubbing off on me as I dwell in the secret place with Him. Because of the work of the Holy Spirit and the Word in my life, I can bear the burdens of others and to forgive with greater ease, regardless of the complaint. Because of the relationship being built with my Father, I can put on love and walk in peace. These are all things we can receive - and need.

The key to receiving these things is prayer and the Word. Verse 16 says,

> *"Let the Word of Christ richly dwell within you and then sing and be melodious in your heart before the Lord."*

It is the Word of God, not just read, but ingested, meditated on and acted upon that brings about ultimate change and growth. God is in the transformation business, with every intention transforming the least of us into His image.

From the very beginning of time God knew the way mankind would be. He knew that sin would reign, that Satan would tempt and that we would make futile efforts in our own strength to be righteous before the Lord and miserably fail.

"I do want to be like you, dad. I want to be like Abba Father." That has become the cry of my heart, and as Christians, it needs to be the cry of all our hearts. The Apostle Paul spoke *"I want to know Christ and the power of his resurrection and the fellowship of sharing in his sufferings,"* (Philippians 3:10). That I may know Him. That I may have intimate relationship with Him. God has such a desire to establish that within us. But it begins with a search to know Him.

Yes, we have become very much like the fathers who have raised us. We have inherited many of their characteristics. It is also true that as we spend time with our Heavenly Father, He will transfer to us His characteristics as well. Will we not develop a heart of love, a desire to serve, a willingness to submit even unto death for the sake of a greater cause over night.

We will change as the Holy Spirit, the life of the Father, flows and functions through our lives! As we allow the Word of Christ to dwell in is, the Logos of the Word, the living word will change us!

What will we look like when we are transformed? Like those with whom we live. The patterns we learn are gained from the ones with whom we dwell. There is no secret to the men and women of God who have walked in great power and authority in their Christian lives. They have learned and focused their entire being on being like the Father. "I want to be like you, dad. Dear Father, I want to be just like you."

To close, let us look again at Matthew 6:6. It says, *"But you, when you pray, go into your room."* Go into your secret place, close yourself off from the world and shut your door. We all have a door that we must shut. Part of the secret is to shut the door on the past. That is determine that "Regardless of where I have been, I have a new Father. He's a good Father. He loves me. I'm going to shut my door, pray to my Father who will hear me in my secret place."

Where is the secret place? Wherever the Father is. Where is the Father? In the hearts of His children. Our Father sees in secret. But you ask, how can He see our words?

Because He is Spiritual, He hears us, He sees us, He knows us because we have His imprint upon our lives. He knows we are being transformed into His image. He who sees in secret will reward you openly. The Apostle Paul proclaims a profound truth. Because of the redemption provided us through the blood of Christ, we are able to see God as through a mirror. As we gaze upon Him, remaining in the secret place, looking intently into His glorious face, we are transformed into the same image. We become like our Father (II Corinthians 3:18).

"I want to be like you, dad. I want the Father's heart." God wants to transform us to such a place that we become fathers like Him, so people will see us and proclaim, "Ah, there is one who has been with the Father."

Appendix 1

Questionnaire for the Father (or Mother)

Introduction:

Dear Dad (or Mom),

As you may know, I am in the process of exploring my life, my past and present, to face and correct difficulties I am experiencing. Some of my hurts relate to our family of origin and our life pattern, of which as my father/mother you are a major part. This questionnaire is designed to get information which may help me in my journey. My focus is not to fix blame, but only to gain understanding which will lead to peace. hope you will help.

Please answer the following questions as openly and candidly as possible. Also, any questions you do not wish to respond to is your prerogative. It is not my intention to pry so as to cause hurt, but to gather information. All your responses will remain between you and I, unless we mutually agree to share it with others.

Thanks for your help.

Love or respectfully,

(your name.)

Questions

I. Since many patterns of behavior and thinking can be seen in past or present generations, please answer the following. These questions will be about your family, including your mom and dad, grandparents and great-grandparents.

    A. As best as you remember, describe your mom/dad/grandma/ grandpa's personality. Please include information such as:

        1. Basic style (passive, aggressive, nervous, angry, loving, kind, gentle, mean, etc.) Please be specific. Mom - Dad, etc. (separate space for each).

_____

_____

_____

_____

_____

_____

_____

_____

        2. What significant memories do you have (or stories told) that provide examples of their personality?

_____

_____

_____

_____

_____

3. What, if any, specific problems/challenges did they have
    in their life? Include vocationally, educationally,
    financially, relationally, physically, socially, other.

_____

_____

_____

_____

_____

_____

_____

_____

B. What was it like for you growing up in your home? Please
    include comments on:
    1. Your relationship with your mom

_____

_____

_____

_____

_____

_____

_____

_____

2. Your relationship with your dad

_____

_____

_____

_____

_____

_____

_____

_____

3. Your relationship with siblings

_____

_____

_____

_____

_____

_____

_____

_____

4. Your relationship with significant others, friends, teachers, etc.

_____

_____

_____

_____

_____

_____

_____

5. What was the atmosphere (happy, sad, angry, fearful, etc) of your home growing up.

_____

_____

_____

_____

_____

_____

_____

C. What personal struggles, challenges did you have in your development? I know this may be hard to answer but your openness could be very helpful – it's up to you.

_____

_____

_____

II. Marriage & Family

A. What were the circumstances surrounding your courtship and marriage of mom/dad. Please include information on:

1. What attracted you to her/him?

_____

_____

_____

_____

_____

2. What challenges did you face?

_____

_____

_____

_____

_____

_____

_____

3. How long did you date before marriage?

_____

_____

_____

_____

_____

_____

_____

B. What was the beginning of the marriage like?

_____

_____

_____

_____

C. Describe the good and bad of your relationship with mom/dad, both the good and bad.

_____

_____

_____

_____

_____

_____

_____

_____

III. You and me.

A. Was my birth planned, or was I a bit of a surprise?

_____

_____

_____

_____

_____

_____

B. What did you think of me as a child?

_____

_____

_____

_____

_____

_____

_____

C. How was our relationship from your perspective?

_____

_____

_____

_____

_____

_____

_____

D. What problems did I have that worried/concerned you about me?

_____

_____

_____

_____

_____

_____

_____

E. What do you think/feel towards me now?

_____

_____

_____

_____

_____

_____

_____

_____

IV. Parenting

A. How would you describe yourself as my parent?

_____

_____

_____

_____

_____

_____

_____

_____

B. If you could have done anything different in the past that might have affected our relationship, what would you have done?

_____

_____

_____

_____

_____

_____

_____

Conclusion

Dad/mom, thank you for completing this. After I have read your responses through, I would like to meet with you to talk about your responses and my reactions. My goal is to strengthen my relationship with you, and to learn enough about you and I to grow and change. If you cannot meet, I will do my best to understand.

Notes to the Searcher

This questionnaire is but a sample. You may want to use this or modify it to suit your needs. However, if you are able to talk face to face with your dad/mom, you might use this as a guide to your discussion. Finally, if you are presently in counseling, listen to the wisdom of your counselor, and only use this tool or make confrontation when he/she believes you are sufficiently ready.

Appendix 2

Life Pattern Questionnaire

After prayer to ask for the Holy Spirit's guidance, answer the questions and complete the questionnaire to the best of your ability.

Life History Questionnaire

The purpose of this questionnaire is to obtain a comprehensive picture of your background. In scientific work, records are necessary, since they permit a more thorough dealing with one's problems, By completing these questions as fully and as accurately as you can, you will facilitate your therapeutic process. You may answer these questions at home or perhaps with a counselor/therapist who can assist you.

It is understandable that you might be concerned about what happens to the information about you, because much or all of this information is highly personal. This information is to be strictly confidential between you and your spiritual mentor.

If you do not desire to answer any questions, merely write, "do not care to answer."

Today's Date: _____

Name: _____

Address: _____

Telephone:_____

Age:_____Occupation:_____

1. With whom are you now living? (list people)

_____

_____

_____

_____

_____

2. Do you live in a house, Hotel, room, apartment, Etc.

_____

_____

_____

_____

Marital Status: (Circle answer)

Single   Engaged   Married   Remarried

Separated   Divorced   Widowed

2. Present Difficulties

(a) State in your own words the nature of your main problems and their duration.

_____

_____

_____

_____

_____

(b) Give a brief account of the history and development of your complaints (from onset to present).

_____

_____

_____

_____

_____

(c) On the scale below please estimate the severity of your problem(s):

Mildly upsetting_____
Moderately upsetting_____
Very upsetting _____
Extremely upsetting _____
Totally upsetting _____
Severely incapacitating_____

(d) Whom have you previously consulted about your present problem(s)?

_____

_____

_____

_____

_____

2. Personal data:
   (a) Date of Birth _____
       Place of Birth _____

   (b) Mother's condition during pregnancy (as far as you know)

_____

_____

_____

_____

_____

   (c) Underline any of the following that applied during your childhood:

   Night terror   bed-wetting
   sleepwalking   thumb-sucking
   nail-biting   stammering
   unhappy childhood   happy childhood
   fears

   (d) Health during childhood

_____

(e) Health during Adolescence

_____

_____

_____

_____

_____

(f) When were you last seen by a doctor?

_____

_____

_____

_____

_____

(g) Any accidents?

_____

_____

_____

_____

_____

(h) List your five main fears:
(1)

_____

_____

(2)

_____

_____

(3)

_____

_____

(4)

_____

_____

(5)

_____

_____

(i) Underline any of the following that apply to you:

Headaches	nightmares	unable to relax
Dizziness	take sedatives	shy with people
fainting spells	alcoholism	over ambitious
palpitations	feel tense	feel panicky
inferiority feeling	stomach trouble	tremors
can't keep a job	no appetite	Depressed
financial problems	bowel disturbance	suicidal ideas
take drugs	concentration problems	fatigue
insomnia	sexual problems	memory problems
can't make friends	home conditions bad	unable to have a good time

(j) Other problems:

_____

_____

(k) Present interests, hobbies, and activities:

_____

_____

(l) How is most of your free time occupied?

_____

_____

(m)What is the last grade of schooling that you completed? ____

(n) Scholastic abilities -- strengths and weaknesses.

_____

_____

_____

(o) Do you make friends easily?
_____Yes _____No
Do you keep them?
_____Yes _____No

3. Occupational data

(a) What sort of work are you doing now?

_____

_____

_____

(b) Kinds of jobs held in the past:

_____

_____

(c) Does your present work satisfy you? (If not, in what ways are you dissatisfied?)

_____

_____

_____

(d) Ambitions: Past: Present:

_____

_____

_____

4. Sex information

(a) Parental attitudes toward sex (i.e., was there sex instruction or discussion in the home?)

_____

_____

_____

(b) When and how did you acquire your first knowledge of sex?

_____

_____

_____

(c) When did you first become aware of your own sexual impulses?

_____

_____

_____

(d) Did you ever experience any anxiety or guilt feelings arising out of sex or masturbation? If "yes" please explain.

_____

_____

(e) Any relevant details regarding your first or subsequent sexual

_____

_____

(f) Is your present sex life satisfactory? (if not, please explain)

_____

_____

(g) Provide information about any significant heterosexual (and/or homosexual) relations:

_____

_____

5. Marital history

(a) How long have you been married?

_____

(b) How long did you know your marriage partner before

engagement?

_____

_____

(c) Husband's / wife's age:_____

(d) Occupation of husband/wife:

_____

_____

_____

(e) Personality of husband or wife (in your own words).

_____

_____

_____

(f) In what areas is there compatibility?

_____

_____

_____

(g) In what areas is there incompatibility?

_____

_____

_____

(h) How do you get along with your in-laws? (this includes brothers and sisters-in-law).

_____

_____

_____

(i) How many children have you had?

_____

(j) Please list their sex and age(s):

_____

_____

_____

Any relevant details regarding miscarriages or abortions?

_____

_____

_____

Give details of an previous marriage(s): Personality of each child: (in your own words)

_____

_____

_____

6. Family data (also Grandfather and Great-grandfather).
   (a) Father: (living or deceased)
   _____

      (1) If deceased, you age at the time of his death:
   _____

      (2) Cause of his death
   _____

      (3) If alive, father's present age:
   _____

      (4) Occupation:
   _____

   (b) Mother: living or deceased?
   _____

(1) If deceased, your age at the time of her death:
_____

(2) Cause of death:
_____

(3) If alive, mother's present age
_____

(4) Occupation:
_____

(c) Siblings

(1)Number of brothers _____

(2)Brother's ages

_____

(3)Number of sisters: _____

(4) Sister's ages

_____

(5) Relationship with siblings:
    a. Past

_____

_____

_____

    b. Present:

_____

_____

_____

(d) Grandparents [Give a description of your grandparent's personality and their attitude toward you (past and present)]:

_____

_____

_____

(e) Great Grandfather: [Give a description of your great-grandfather's personality and his attitude toward you (past and present)]:

_____

_____

_____

(f) Give a description of your mother's personality and her attitude toward you (past and present).

_____

_____

_____

(g) In what ways were you punished by your parents as a child?

_____

_____

_____

(h) Give an impression of your home atmosphere (i.e., the home in which you grew up. Mention state of compatibility between parents and between parents and children).

_____

_____

(i). Were you able to confide in you parents?

_____

(j). If you have a step-parent, give your age when parent remarried _____.

(k) Give an outline of your religious training:

_____

_____

_____

(l) If you were not brought up by your parents, who did bring you up and between what years?

_____

_____

(m) Has anyone (parents, relatives, friends) ever interfered in your life? How?

_____

_____

_____

(n) Who are the most important people in your life?

_____

_____

_____

(o) Does any member of your family suffer from alcoholism, epilepsy or anything which can be considered a "mental disorder?" Give details.
Are there any other members of the family about whom information regarding illness, etc., is relevant?

_____

_____

_____

(p) Are there any other members of the family about whom information regarding illness, etc., is relevant?

_____

_____

_____

(q) Recount any fearful or distressing experiences not previously mentioned.

_____

_____

_____

_____

(r) List any situations that make you feel particularly anxious.

_____

_____

_____

(s) List any situations which make you feel calm or relaxed.

_____

_____

_____

(t) Have you ever lost control (i.e., temper or crying or aggression)? If so, describe:

_____

_____

_____

7. Please add any information not covered by this questionnaire that may aid your counselor in understanding and helping you.

_____

_____

_____

Stan E. DeKoven, Ph.D.

Non-Christian Spiritual Experience Inventory

Use the rest of this page and the attached blank page to give a word picture of yourself as you would be described:

(a) by yourself

_____

_____

_____

(b) by your spouse (if married)

_____

_____

_____

(c) by your best friend

_____

_____

_____

(d) by someone who dislikes you.

_____

_____

_____

Addendum

A Wider Application

Historically, curses were not brought upon individuals or families alone, but the evidence of destructive patterns can be seen in groups, communities, church and nations. Some Christian writers have made note of this fact in their writings (Dawson, 1989), and it deserves some further elaboration. Truly, our strategy for the deliverance and healing of the nations must include a warfare strategy and must focus on the prophecy of Malachi 4:3-6.

> *"Remember the law of my servant Moses, the decrees and laws I gave him at Horeb for all Israel. See, I will send you the prophet Elijah before that great and dreadful day of the LORD comes. He will turn the hearts of the fathers to their children, and the hearts of the children to their fathers; or else I will come and strike the land with a curse."*

Every community, city, and nation has a personality. Every church faces unique challenges, temptations and trials designed to destroy the worth of that institution. Much of that personality and the problems seen can be traced to the history of that institution. An awareness of the history, areas of sin, cursed vs. blessed behaviors of the past that may have opened the community to the attacks of the enemy need to be fully understood. Thus, in areas of specific vulnerability, positive action can be taken.

What's in a Name?

The names given to various communities can provide a clue to the history, and thus areas of potential oppression. However, more often it is the labels given to communities that tend to speak to the problems of that community, church, or nation. For example:

San Diego, my home town, is a part of "California casual." It is known as a laid back, conservative, recreation oriented community. Established initially as a Spanish mission, it is one of the only major seaports to never experience a revival. Even Billy Graham vowed to never return to San Diego because of the apathy and lack of support from area churches. This apathetic "spirit", "spirit of play, and leisure" remains prevalent and a major problem for area churches. There is a lack of commitment to the local churches, significant church hopping and spiritual thrill seeking.

Of course, as with most of California, the Spaniards and the other settlers displaced the native Indians, removing the boundaries (Deut 27:17, etc.). Ultimately, the issues of the personality of the city must be dealt with by the power of God, through the prayer of agreement in a united and sustained effort of evangelism and the ministry of the Word of God.

Another example can be seen in the "life" of a local church. This church was at one time a most dynamic evangelistic church impacting the community. Over a period of 20 years this church had several incidents of gross sin, repeated without exposure to anyone but the leadership. Each time the sins were covered up rather than dealt with in a biblical way. Why of the same type of sin was repeated over and over by different families in the church is a mystery. Ultimately, this church has virtually died, partially due to this problem of sin and the church's unwillingness to embrace a changing community. How many other churches may be attacked and thwarted due to generational patterns that are unknown or unconfessed?

Territorial Warfare

Recently, there has been teaching on and rallies for the "tearing down of strongholds" of territorial spirits in a given region. Proponents of this type of ministry include highly respected ministers, including John Dawson (1989) and Peter Wagner. I am certainly not in a position to evaluate effectively the effectiveness of this ministry effort. In principle, addressing generational patterns through awareness, confession of sin, repentance, forgiveness, and restoration through the power of God's Word can make an impact on a community. However, rather than "cursing the darkness" it is better to light a candle through the proclamation of the Gospel of Jesus Christ which can to reduce or nullify some of the demonic influences in a region. Most importantly, our prayer should be as Paul's prayer for the great Church,

"For this reason, ever since I heard about your faith in the Lord Jesus and your love for all saints, I have not stopped giving thanks for you, remembering you in my prayers. I keep asking that the God of our Lord Jesus Christ, the glorious Father, may give you the Spirit of wisdom and revelation, so that you may know him better. I pray also that the eyes of your heart may be enlightened in order that you may know the hope to which he has called you, the riches of his glorious inheritance in the saints, and his incomparably great power for us who believe. That power is like the working of his mighty strength, which he exerted in Christ when he raised him from the dead and seated him at his right hand in the heavenly realms, far above all rule and authority, power and dominion, and every title that can be given, not only in the present age but also in the one to come. And God placed all things under his feet and appointed him to be head over everything for the church, which is his body, the fullness of him who fills everything in every way, " (Ephesians 1:11-23).

241

Bibliography

Anderson, Neil T. *The Bondage Breaker*. Eugene Oregon: Harvest House. 1990.

Steps to Freedom in Christ. La Habra: Freedom in Christ Ministries, 1993.

Bohac, Joseph J. *Human Development: A Christian Perspective*. Ramona, CA: Vision Publishing. 1993.

Dawson, John. *Taking Our Cities for God*. Lake Mary: Creation House. 1989.

DeKoven, Stan. *40 Days to the Promise: A Way Through the Wilderness*. Ramona: Vision Publishing. 1993.

DeKoven, Stan. *Journey to Wholeness: Restoration of the Soul*. Ramona: Vision Publishing. 1993.

DeKoven, Stan. *Grief Relief*. San Diego: Christian Service Publishing. 1990.

DeKoven, Stan. *Twelve Step to Wholeness*. Ramona, CA: Vision Publishing. 1989.

Hickey, Marilyn. *Break the Generational Curse*.

Jarrard, Doug. *Freedom From Iniquity*. Lawrenceville, GA: Vision Christian World Ministries. 1994.

Johnson, M. *Spiritual Warfare for the Wounded.* Ann Arbor: Servant Publishing.

Litchfield, Bruce. *Doctoral Dissertation.* "Sexual Dysfunctions." Vision Christian College. 1990.

McClung, Floyd. *Holiness and the Spirit of the Age.* Eugene: Harvest House Publishers. 1990.

Payne, Leonne. *Restoring the Christian Soul Through Healing Prayer.* Chicago: Crossway Books. 1991.

Prince, Derek. *Blessing or Curse – You Can Choose.* Grand Rapids: Baker Books.

Robeson, Jerry and Carol. *Strongman's His Name: What's His Game?*

Sanford, John, and Sanford, R. *The Renewal of the Mind.* Victory House Publishing. 1991

Sherrer, Q. and Garlock, R. *A Women's Guide to Spiritual Warfare.* Publisher unknown.

White, T. *Breaking Strongholds: How Spiritual Warfare Sets Captives Free.* Vine Books, Servant Publications. 1993

The Teaching Ministry of Dr. Stan DeKoven

Dr. DeKoven conducts seminars based on his books in Practical Christian Living nationally and internationally. He is available for limited engagements for church seminars, retreats and conferences. For a complete listing of topics and books, you can contact:

Dr. Stan DeKoven, President

Vision International University

Walk in Wisdom Seminars

1115 D Street

Ramona, CA 92065

(760) 789-4700

Other Books by Dr. DeKoven
on similar topics:

Grief Relief

Journey to Wholeness: Restoration of the Soul

40 Days to the Promise: A Way Through the Wilderness

Marriage and Family Life: A Christian Perspective

Crisis Counseling

On Belay! Introduction to Christian Counseling

Family Violence: Patterns of Destruction

www.ingramcontent.com/pod-product-compliance
Lightning Source LLC
Chambersburg PA
CBHW031937031025
33557CB00046B/1163